GRANDPARENTING

A Guide Through the BY Joys and Struggles

GRACE

Irene M. Endicott

BROADMAN
& HOLMAN
PUBLISHERS

Nashville, Tennessee

Printed in the United States of America

4261-49
0-8054-6149-3

Dewey Decimal Classification: 306.874
Subject Heading: GRANDPARENT AND CHILD
Library of Congress Card Catalog Number: 94-12583

Library of Congress Cataloging-in-Publication Data

Endicott, Irene M.
   Grandparenting by grace : a guide through the joys and struggles / Irene
M. Endicott.
      p. cm.
   ISBN 0-8054-6149-3
   1. Grandparenting. 2. Grandparenting—Religious aspects —Christian-
ity. 3. Grandparent and child. I. Title.
HQ759.9.E52   1994
306.874'5—dc20   94-12583
                                                                       CIP

To my husband, Bill, the best grandpa I know;
to my twelve perfect grandchildren,
and to all who want to learn more about
grandparenting by grace.

G Grace—in the beginning and to the end
R Responsibility—role modeling, teaching, praying
A Availability—helpful, ready, standing by
N Needs—meeting theirs and yours
D Devotion—committed, well-grounded
P Perseverance—standing firm, confident
A Assurance—faith
R Reward—humility
E Energy—happy, fun-loving, surprising
N Neutral—cooperative, nonconfrontational
T Trust—understanding, accepting
I Involved—connected, good company
N Nurturing—loving, caring, touching
G Grace—a legacy for the generations

CONTENTS

PREFACE

Little hands clasped tightly under a chubby chin, a grandchild's eyes glistened with excitement as Grandma opened the box and exclaimed, "Oh, it's beautiful! Just what I needed!"

Presents, especially those from grandchildren, have great value. Their value is not rooted in cost or beauty but in the giver of the gift. Gratitude overflows our hearts.

In a lifetime, we receive countless valuable presents. One, however, is given more often than any other. It is impossible to place a value on it or to adequately thank the Giver. It is the gift of grace from God.

As we grow older and reflect upon the years that have gone by so fast, we can clearly see God's grace manifested in our lives as "just what we needed." And we need it today more than ever.

Grace is the biblical concept upon which *Grandparenting by Grace* is based. The Bible teaches wonderful principles about God's saving and sustaining grace. It's a free gift! We can't earn it! We don't deserve it! God's grace is sufficient for all of our needs in this life, and because of His great love for us, we have the hope of eternal life with Him! You will find a Grace Principle and accompanying Scripture at the end of each chapter.

This book represents many years of research into the joys and struggles of grandparenting, thousands of interviews with grandparents aged twenty-eight and older; plus hope, encouragement, and instruction for grandparents from the Bible. As the grandmother of twelve perfect grandchildren, I know the joy of this season of life. Because grandchildren come with parents, I also know the pain and sorrow of changing and lost relationships.

There is no grandparenting university. We must learn from each other and from God's holy Word. Reading *Grandparenting by Grace*, you will be affirmed of your central place in the family, as well as your value to your family and to God. You will learn new and innovative ways to become a more effective and loving grandparent, how to have more fun with your grandchildren even if they live far away, and how to cope with the difficult times.

Old truths from the Scriptures become new again as we seek to grandparent by God's grace.

ॐ

ACKNOWLEDGMENTS

Special thanks to
- ❖ Avery Willis, Roy Edgemon, and Jay Johnston, men of vision who saw the need.
- ❖ The staff of the Discipleship and Family Development Department of the Sunday School Board of the Southern Baptist Convention for their encouragement and prayers.
- ❖ Vicki Crumpton, my editor at Broadman and Holman Publishers, for believing that God would do a work through me, and for her warm professionalism and compassion for contemporary grandparents.
- ❖ Each grandparent who shared a personal story so that someone else might better understand the joys and struggles of this season of life.

❦

GRANDPARENTING IN THE NINETIES

God does not require resumés, even from grandparents. That's because He knows everything. He was the childbirth coach for each of us. He knows even the number of hairs on our heads.

He was there as we grew up. He saw the first step, heard the first word, answered the first prayer. He witnessed our education. He blessed our marriage. He wrote the rules by which, hopefully, we raised our children.

Now here we are. Growing older, growing wiser. Our children's children call us "Nana," "Umpa," "Grammie," "Gramps," "Meemah," or "Peepah." Our resumé may not show us as qualified for the title.

In part 1, we will seek His instruction in this important role. We'll see how much the job has changed since the time of your grandparents and mine, how grandparents themselves have changed, and the ways those changes affect the entire family.

I hope you will experience a flood of precious memories of your own grandparents now as I introduce you to one of God's great gifts to me . . . my grandmother.

℮

Chapter 1

THE ROLE OF GRANDPARENT

Sitting at the hand-hewn table in the corner of her kitchen, a blanket around my shoulders against the morning chill, I watched my Grandma Burch at the old wood stove, rubbing her strong hands together over the crackling fire as she lovingly prepared a breakfast fit for a king. Breakfast for my parents, for me, and any number of my ten brothers and sisters. Surely she had prepared thousands of such meals for her own seventeen children born in that little log house built by my grandpa in Deer Lodge, Montana, at the turn of the century.

I recall the intoxicating aromas of thick bacon crisping, fresh honey in the warming oven, and hot biscuits in the oven below. And the coffee! Ahhh, the coffee! I was just a little girl of seven or eight, and mother had said I couldn't have any. But I was always the first one up, and Grandma and I had coffee together, mine mostly sugar and cream.

Grandma spoke quietly and gently to me in the stillness of those early Montana mornings. I remember feeling honored that such a great lady would take time with me. I listened. Grandma's wisdom and Christian witness went deep into my soul, a wellspring from which I could draw all of my life. I don't remember Grandma's words from over fifty years ago, but I remember the principles and values that were as much a part of her as the gentle look of love in her eyes and the warmth of her hugs.

Grandma Burch was typical of most grandparents in the thirties and forties, revered and honored by their families, personifying the role as God has ordained it: counselor, historian, friend, and living witness of the faith.

Grandmother. Just saying the name brings a flood of treasured memories for most of us.

Grandfather. A grand name that stands for respect, security, strength, knowledge, and love.

We *live* and *love* the role of grandparent. There are almost 60 million of us today, and that number is growing fast. Half of the adults aged forty-five to fifty-nine and 83 percent of those aged sixty and older are grandparents. Baby boomers moving into these age groups will drive grandparent growth into the next century. By 2005, 76 million of us may be grandparents, an increase of 26 percent from 1992.[1]

Thankfully, most grandparents are experiencing this season of life as God intended, relaxing, studying, traveling, enjoying the fruits of many years of labor *and* spending time with grandchildren who are being raised in a healthy, loving home environment.

Proverbs 17:6 tells us "Children's children are a crown to the aged." Unhappily though, for many grandparents in the nineties, their crowns have been tarnished as they witness breakdowns in young families and the excruciating pain and loss endured by their grandchildren. For these grandparents, the role has changed and will never be the same.

Today, grandparents in greater numbers than ever before in our history are standing in the gap for their adult children for the sake of their grandchildren. More than 3 million children in America are being raised by their grandparents.[2] Experts say that the census figure of 3.3 million is probably more like 5–7 million and will be 13–14 million by the year 2000.

Countless other thousands of grandparents are taking back into their homes pieces of breaking and broken families or providing financial assistance, transportation, food, and other vital support to their children and grandchildren. Still others are grappling with the loss and pain that comes with divorce, bad habits, stress, and many other tragedies resulting from bad choices and other circumstances in the lives of adult kids.

How did this happen? We remember the loving grandparents of the thirties and forties. They were made for loving. That was their job. They were always there in times of trouble or sorrow, for advice or just a simple pat on the shoulder to say that all was well. It was not uncommon for several generations to live in harmony under the same roof.

Then came World War II. Grandparents took jobs in factories, shipyards, and offices as sons and daughters served their country in the military. Times were difficult during the war, but family unity was still strong. When the war ended, many grandparents stayed in the work force. Grandparents and great-grandparents who had survived the Great Depression and the war welcomed the peaceful Eisenhower years of the fifties, when it was important to go to church, divorce was a bad word, abortion was unthinkable, and we thought the family unit was unbreakable. Little did we know that the smoldering undercurrent of that decade would erupt in the turbulent sixties.

It has been said of the sixties that "if you remember them, you weren't there." But if you were a grandparent in the sixties, you remember them. You witnessed the changes in morality, the revolt against authority, the "God is dead" and "Free Love" mentality that ruled this era.

The seventies brought an epidemic of substance abuse and deeper erosion of family values. Throughout the eighties, America's grandparents witnessed a decade of greed, lack of commitment, and perverted lifestyles. They watched helplessly as the numbers of abused children and grandchildren soared. This is what is happening in the nineties:

CURRENT TRENDS

❖ Drug and alcohol abuse have invaded even Christian homes, leaving the very lives of grandchilden in jeopardy.

❖ Divorce and lack of commitment are ravaging the fabric of the family as more than 60 percent of marriages fail. Eighty percent of those spouses will marry again at least once and are raising our grandchildren.

❖ Homosexual men and women have gained acceptance and power in today's society, threatening the God-ordained family.

❖ Adult children and grandchildren are abandoning their faith in God and their values to follow false prophets, even Satan.

❖ Young grandparents are accepting the responsibility of raising infants born to teenage daughters and sons.

❖ Shameful abuse statistics rise every year, while millions go unreported. One-third of initial child abuse calls result in informal arrangements with a family member, usually a grandparent.

❖ Increased incidence of young parents' suicide, imprisonment, mental illness, and death by accident also lead the list of trends affecting grandparents and grandchildren.

❖ Contact between grandparent and grandchild has been broken due to divorce, remarriage, or the death of a parent. Grandparents seeking visitation or custody of grandchildren is a growing phenomenon in America.

❖ Long marriages are being strained to the breaking point because of Grandma's involvement in the lives of grandchildren and their parents.

If these trends have not touched your life, they have touched the life of a neighbor, a family member, or friend. But nineties grandparents are learning from the past, and we know more today than we did forty or fifty years ago. We're trying to keep our perspective in this important job, help young families and restore the joy of the grandparent role.

Why? Because we love our grandchildren, and we will always want the best for our children. We want to better understand our current role and how we can live it in faith and love.

We know that we can make a difference in our grandchildren's lives.

THE SIGNIFICANCE OF THE ROLE

- ❖ Grandparents are the central core of the family. We partner with parents in teaching the plan of salvation to our grandchildren.
- ❖ We undergird our grandchildren with faithful prayer.
- ❖ We are witnesses to share how God has proven faithful to His people and to our family specifically.
- ❖ We are the family historian, holding the keys to learning about family roots and experiences for the generations to come.
- ❖ We have fun with our grandchildren and build their self-esteem.
- ❖ We are a safe refuge for our grandchildren in times of trouble.
- ❖ We are a soft shoulder in sorrow and the encourager of new beginnings.
- ❖ We are wise, nonjudgmental counselors of our grandchildren.
- ❖ We bless our grandchildren by honoring their achievements and showing compassion for their losses.
- ❖ We represent stability to young families dealing with change.

God's Plan for Grandparents

Although there is no "job description" for grandparents in the Bible, certain passages define what God had in mind when He created the position. I think the best example is Deuteronomy 4:9: "Only be careful, and watch yourselves closely so that you do not forget the things your eyes have seen or let them slip from your heart as long as you live. Teach them to your children and to their children after them."

What does that mean?

"Be careful, and watch yourselves closely" implies the seriousness of the grandparent role. It is not one to be taken lightly or haphazardly, but with diligence and self-discipline. This is a revelation to some grandparents who have never considered themselves as central or important to the family.

"Do not forget the things your eyes have seen or let them slip from your heart." All Christian grandparents have that overflowing of gratitude in our hearts for the thousands upon thousands of blessings we have received by God's grace during our long lives. We have witnessed His handiwork, His love, His forgiveness, and so much more that is our privilege to pass on to our children.

"As long as you live" reminds us that as long as God gives life and breath, our job continues. We cannot let our guard down. We must not miss an opportunity to witness to our children and grandchildren, for time is short and there is much to say and share.

"Teach them to your children and to their children after them." We are admonished to teach, not as a professional might be able, but in our own unique ways, with God-given gifts and methods meant just for our family. This portion of the Scripture carries with it the heaviest of responsibility, for God does not say that we can teach if we want to or that it is all right if we don't. This is a mandate for grandparents that cannot be ignored.

Proverbs 17:6, "Children's children are a crown to the aged, and parents are the pride of their children," is God's indication of mutual reward in this job. More than that, it is His expectation for the conduct of all parties.

Do you think of your grandchildren as a crown? They are. Grandchildren are an awesome gift from God. Remember though, that even royalty must acknowledge that there are responsibilities that accompany the crown they wear. So it is for us.

The Scriptures are filled with affirmations of blessing for us and for our grandchildren as we covenant with God in the grandparenting role. An especially beautiful example is Psalm 103:17–18: "But from everlasting to everlasting the Lord's love is with those who fear him, and his righteousness with their children's children—with those who keep his covenant and remember to obey his precepts."

GRANDMOTHER AND GRANDFATHER

Teacher, pastor, and grandfather, C. Ferris Jordan offers this perspective on the differences in the role of grandmother and grandfather:

> God planned that children have grandmothers and grandfathers. His wise design recognizes that children need the unique impact that can be made by grandparents of each gender. If grandmothers and grandfathers were making identical contributions, there would be no need for both. Each grandparent is an individual with his or her own personal history, personality, abilities, and interpersonal relationship skills. These differences can enrich grandparents' combined efforts as they relate to their grandchildren.

Not all children are blessed with four grandparents who are vitally involved in their lives. On the other hand, some children have four grandparents plus step-grandparents, all of whom are making positive contributions and constitute a powerful support system. Even if you are the only grandparent available to or interested in your grandchild(ren), it is important that you fulfill your role well.

Differences in grandmother and grandfather roles can be very positive, complementing or sometimes buffering each other. For example, it is generally accepted that by nature, grandmothers are the nurturers, peacemakers, and sympathizers, while grandfathers are the advisors and storytellers. That may not always be the case at your house. Perhaps you are more the coach and your spouse, the cheerleader. Grandma may be the saver, Grandpa the spender! It doesn't matter who does what. The important thing is that the differences work together toward the common goal of being the best grandparents we can be.

In the following list, see which ones fit you and your spouse, and then ask yourself whether those differences are working together for good:

Nurturer	Provider
Peacemaker	Hero
Cheerleader	Coach
Sympathizer	Advisor
Playmate	Adventurer
Hugger	Talker
Cook	Eater
Teacher	Planner
Spender	Saver
Reader	Storyteller
Communicator	Demonstrator

—

Inherent in the grandparent role are potential hazards that we don't even like to think about, but they do happen. While we will carefully examine them more carefully in later chapters, here are a few:

Overinvolvement	Unhealthy love
Underinvolvement	Spoiling
Meddling	Discouragement
Getting feelings hurt	Showing favoritism

But grandparents don't think about hazards! We're having too much fun with our grandkids. Count the blessings!

Laughter	Caring
Witnessing	Giving
Sharing	Being part of their lives
Learning together	Watching them grow
Loving	Cheering their achievements
Surprises	Applauding their good looks

In short, we've got the best job in the world!

STEREOTYPES

Living out the best job in the world hasn't always been easy. In the past, a grandparent might have walked into church on Sunday morning to have a friend ask, "How are those precious grandkids?" Answer? "Just fine!" No matter what was going on in the family, that's what grandparents were expected to say—yesterday.

Today, worldly expectations of the grandparenting role are being exposed. So many grandparents are in the parent role with their grandkids today that grandparents facing challenges are talking more freely about them and seeking the encouragement and resources that exist. Grandparents have freed themselves of the stereotypical role of grandparents who stayed on the sidelines in the lives of their children and grandchildren. The role is markedly different today, as this list of past stereotypical grandparent roles illustrates:

THEN AND NOW

Forties and Fifties Grandparents	_Nineties Grandparents_
Older	Getting younger every day
In rocking chair	On cruise ship
Never speak out on issues	Activist
Stay at home	Working
Free babysitter	Setting boundaries
Dependent on others	Independent
Easygoing	Stressed
Retired	Second or third career
Available anytime	Busy

IT'S A NEW DAY!

Lifestyles of grandparents have changed in the nineties, and so has our image of the "typical" grandparent. Today's grandparents are discovering new ways to be involved in their families, their churches, and in their communities. Grandma's working out. She's healthier. She's volunteering for a good cause, shopping at the mall, or traveling the world. Grandpa is living longer, is well-informed, more involved. There is a welcome resurgence in the numbers of senior-aged men becoming more active in church and community affairs, bringing much needed leadership and wisdom that can come only from experience.

Not all of the changes in grandparents are positive. Lack of grandparent participation in the family is a heartache for some parents. Some grandparents choose not to grandparent because they are jaded from the past. They say hurtful things like, "I raised my kids. You raise yours!" or "Don't call me 'Grandma'!"

Other changing grandparent attitudes account for meddling, spoiling grandchildren, and competing with other grandparents. The sad fallout from such attitudes is that grandchildren lose the most. We will examine these and other serious situations in later chapters.

How Am I Doing?

A grandparent at a conference at which I was speaking told me that if he had known how wonderful his grandchildren were going to be, he would have been nicer to their parents. Another likened grandparenting to getting a second chance at being a good parent. Still another said it's like a reward for a job well done raising their own children.

How do you feel about it? Have some of the changing lifestyles and attitudes affected you? Are you pleased with your grandparenting season? How do others see you in this role? What changes might you make? Such questions can evoke a wide variety of responses because grandparenting is so individual, so personal. It is healthy, however, to evaluate our progress in this important job. Think about these questions in light of your own circumstances. Honest answers may be difficult or even painful; but they might also open new avenues to more godly, loving, and effective grandparenting:

1. Have I accepted this role as part of God's plan for my life?
2. What is my understanding of my role in the family?
3. What do other family members expect of me?
4. Am I realistic about what I can accomplish in this role?
5. What have I learned from the past that makes me a better grandparent?
6. Do I undergird my children and grandchildren with faithful prayer?
7. How do my children view me as a grandparent?
8. How do I show consistency in this role?
9. How have I shown love to my grandchildren even when they are unlovable?
10. How am I using my gifts to benefit my grandchildren?
11. Am I a safe refuge for my children and grandchildren?

12. What might be some ways I am overinvolved in my grand-children's lives?
13. What might be some ways I need to be more involved in my grandchildren's lives?
14. What do my grandchildren think of me?
15. In what areas might I improve as a grandparent?
16. Do I grandparent according to God's Word?
17. What do I like least about this job?
18. How am I having fun as a grandparent?
19. Do I confront problem relationships with love and pa-tience?
20. How do I receive criticism?
21. Is there a need to ask for forgiveness from my adult child or grandchild?
22. How am I instilling a sense of family in my grandchildren?
23. How am I keeping a loving, caring link with grandchildren who live far away?
24. Am I faithfully modeling Christ for my grandchildren?
25. Is the legacy I will pass on temporary or eternal?

GRACE PRINCIPLE:

God's grace sustains us.

For the Lord God is a sun and shield; the Lord gives grace and glory; no good thing does He withhold from those who walk uprightly.

— Psalm 84:11, NASB

Now that we have a better understanding of who we are as grandparents, let's concentrate on how to be good ones.

☙

Chapter 2

LEARNING TO GRANDPARENT

Your answers to the questions at the end of chapter 1 may signal a need to learn more about being a grandparent. Perhaps you are expecting your very first grandchild soon or *(perish the thought)* you have no prospects on the horizon but want to be ready. Maybe the whole idea of becoming a grandparent makes you feel uneasy because you had no role models in your growing-up years or you are just not sure you are ready for this.

Relax. No instruction manual came with any of our twelve perfect grandchildren either. Like parenting, grandparenting is a job you learn as you go. So—here we go!

WHAT DOES IT TAKE TO QUALIFY?

A spouse, a child, and a baby.

That may seem oversimplified, but it is true. If you and your spouse had a baby and that baby has a baby, you are a grandparent! How grand you become after you are qualified is what this book is all about.

Biological qualification may come unexpectedly and too early today as very young children present parents with grandchildren. Or it can come late in life as more and more couples wait longer to have a baby.

Qualification as a grandparent in the nineties can come from other than biological sources, such as a new marriage of an adult child to a spouse with children. Then there are the blurred lines of qualification when we marry again and his or her kids have kids who may or may not call you "Grandma" or "Grandpa." It sounds complicated, but it really isn't when you remember no matter how you qualify as a grandparent, to concentrate *not* on those circumstances but on being a good grandparent to the child.

How Can I Learn to Be a Good Grandparent?

It's easier for some than for others. Most of us have a natural desire or drive to grandparent. We look forward to it as a logical transition from parenting. Some can hardly wait! One lady bothered her two sons so often about the fact that she had no grandchildren, one son asked, "Well, Mom, shouldn't we get married first?"

Several of the qualities of a good grandparent follow.

A good grandparent has a good attitude—willing to exchange a few red, black, brown, or blonde hairs for gray ones; willing to wait for the blessed event and to accept it when it happens.

A good grandparent is mature—maturity has less to do with age than with understanding the responsibilities of the role.

A good grandparent is cheerful—a pleasure to be around, creating a happy spirit in everything said and done.

A good grandparent is available—when the family has needs.

A good grandparent has a good memory—to remember what it was like to be a parent and to remember those people from the past who made valuable contributions as role models. Observation and imitation of good grandparent role models help to mold the grandparent we become.

A good grandparent is courageous—in a world that is a dangerous place for millions of children who desperately need the strength and assurance of a courageous grandparent.

A good grandparent is flexible—with behavior patterns, understanding that things and people change and that grandparents were never meant to replace parents.

A good grandparent has stamina—for staying power during life situations which require your best, even "for better or worse, in sickness and in health."

A good grandparent is loving—different from parental love. A deeper love born of experience, of trial and error; a connected love that is peaceful and nonjudgmental.

Notice any mention of good looks or good bank balances? No. That's because they don't matter in a good grandparent. What matters is what is inside— who we are in Christ. Inherent in the Christian grandparent is the desire to please God by every thought, word, and deed. Worldly forces, however, can confuse and dissuade Christian grandparents from that desire, leaving some wondering if what is happening to them and their family is normal.

Normal Grandparenting

Scholars have been trying to define "normal" for generations. What is normal for one may not be normal for another. What is normal grandparenting?

- ❖ Is it what is appropriate?
- ❖ Is it what is culturally correct?
- ❖ Is it what most people do?

I suggest that normal is what is best for you and your family.

Grandparents who prayerfully employ the qualities of a good grandparent, in harmony with the needs and desires of their individual family members, will achieve the degree of normalcy right for them.

AFFAIRS OF THE HEART

It happens. There you are, trying to be the best grandparent you can be to each grandchild, and whether you recognize it or not, one or two of those precious ones steals your heart away. Grandfathers, for example, universally accept and love both granddaughters and grandsons. But very often, the granddaughter will occupy a special corner of Grandpa's heart. She runs right to Grandpa when he comes through the door. In little ways, she lets him know how very important he is to her, and Grandpa melts. "I don't know what it is," he says. "My granddaughter and I just have something special."

Good grandfathers are easy for little girls to love. One youngster said, "My grandfather is more relaxed than my dad. He has more time for me. I ramble on about nothing and he just smiles and gives me a big, warm hug. My grandfather understands me. I love him so much. I don't know what I'd do without him."

Good grandfathers are also lovable because they provide a male role model for the granddaughter who has no dad or other men in her life. Their genuine caring, attentiveness, and availability can present a more loving impression of a Christian man to that granddaughter who may have experienced only negative models.

Accordingly, grandmothers can have a special affinity for a grandson, especially the son of their son—that one who looks so much like her own child when he was little and who seems to gravitate toward Grandma, filled with love for her.

One grandmother told me, "I love all of my grandchildren equally. I have no favorite. That wouldn't be right. It's just that John seems to prefer to be with me. He's so much like his father!"

It's normal to have warm feelings for one who reminds us so much of our own kin and who rekindles wonderful memories just by being alive. Remember, though, that a good grandparent maintains a proper balance in the expression of those feelings, especially if there are siblings.

Good Grandparenting Saves Lives

Some grandparents bring a lot of baggage to the role—not distorted images of what a good grandparent is, reflections of the past shrouded in conflict, deprivation or confused relationships. Learning to be a healthy, giving, loving grandparent can lift up those who have a skewed view of the job to a whole new and productive chapter in their lives—not one filled with joy such as they have never known, sharing as they have never before experienced it, caring for someone else as no one ever cared for them.

Grandparenting can be a life-saving season—yours and someone else's—as we can see from these testimonies: "I didn't know I could love anybody as much as I love my grandchild;" "I didn't know anybody could love me the way my grandchild does;" "Being here for my grandbaby has given me a reason for living."

A Good Grandparent Is Immortal

Grandma Jane amended her will, allocating certain amounts of money to the great-great-great-grandchildren of her grandchildren. She said she was seeking immortality. Allocating monies to future generations, however, will prove far less significant to Jane's immortality than a legacy of good grandparenting. Lasting "fame" should come from teaching, witnessing to, praying for, and encouraging the grandchild who will carry on the good work.

The apostle Paul makes a remark about Timothy's mother and grandmother as having had a positive or godly effect on the young man Timothy (2 Tim. 1:5). The passage doesn't tell us if Timothy actually ever knew his grandmother, only that she was a godly woman and that she passed her faith on to her daughter, Eunice, Timothy's mother. Throughout Scripture, grandparents are seen as providing a rich heritage of godliness.

Immortality (lasting fame) is a worthy goal, though few, if any, actually achieve it. As with so many other goals in life, it is the striving that counts. The motivation for immortality as a grandparent, we assume, is a positive one. The measure of its achievement will not be in dollars but in the heritage of godliness we leave behind.

You didn't realize you were that important, did you? Well, you are. As we learned in chapter 1, a grandparent is central to the family. I encourage you to dedicate the rest of your life to learning how to be a good one. The Author and Finisher of the faith will bless you and yours abundantly.

GRACE PRINCIPLE:

Good grandparents learn by God's grace.

Each one should retain the place in life that the Lord assigned to him and to which God has called him.
— 1 Corinthians 7:17

Now, let's look at how good grandparents can live this role in partnership with parents.

ℰ

Chapter 3

PARTNERING
WITH PARENTS

Seventeen-year-old James, a B+ student, was gifted with a good mind and a personality that made him one of the more popular boys at his high school. He had always been a "strong-willed" child bent on doing his own thing, which led to shouting matches with his parents about situations such as missing weeknight curfews, spending money, and doing household chores.

James knew he had one sure ally in the world: Grampa Mullins. His earliest memories were of time spent with his grandfather, either perched on the bench in the workshop listening to tall tales of his grandfather's own childhood or taking a drive in the pickup, pouring out his problems, hopes, and dreams to the one person in the family he felt really heard him. Grampa Mullins always had the right answer. James knew his grandfather loved him unconditionally and would do just about anything for him.

What a gift a grandparent can be to a young person unsteady on the path of life!

It was the ideal grandparent/grandson relationship until James needed a thousand dollars. He knew where to go. Grampa Mullins listened attentively to the plea for "only a thousand" for a computer that would help him with his studies and that he could take on to college.

Grampa eagerly gave the thousand dollars. After all, it was James! And this would really help his future.

When James' parents found out, they were incredulous.

"Dad, how could you? How could you give James all that money without talking to us? Do you know what you've done? Now he'll never learn the principles we've been trying so hard to teach him about earning his own money and being responsible for his decisions. Thanks a lot, Dad!"

One year went by, and it was a very lonely year for Grampa Mullins. His daughter and son-in-law hadn't called or invited him over. Gramps decided to call his grandson at college to see how he was doing and to negotiate repayment of the loan. James did not return his grandfather's call. James was aware of his parents' wrath over the thousand-dollar loan and knew he had no way of repaying it. There was no paperwork, no promissory note, so high-spirited James figured he didn't owe his grandfather anyway. After all, his grandfather loved him unconditionally!

What did Grampa Mullins do wrong?

❖ He did not consult with his grandson's parents prior to giving the loan.
❖ He did not set conditions for repayment of the loan.
❖ He forgot that unconditional love for a grandchild carries with it responsibility.

Grandparents must not usurp the authority of the parent. When our children marry, the authority structure changes. Grandparents become a source of counsel. If a grandchild seeks our counsel, we must know that they first sought the counsel of their parents and what counsel was given. This is a rule to follow not only when dealing with money issues but in all areas as we partner with parents.

Grampa Mullins chose a most unusual way to solve his dilemma. He wrote a letter to James forgiving the debt. The letter said,

Dear James,

I hereby forgive your debt to me in the amount of $1,000. I want you to know that I do not blame you for asking for the money. I know you felt you needed it. The fault was mine in giving the money without first checking with your parents and without making you accountable for payment of the loan. This has been a good lesson for me. I hope and pray it also has been a good lesson for you.

Love, Grampa

This was a head-scratcher for James at first. As he thought about it, though, and talked with his parents and his grandfather, James learned lessons he will never forget.

When James' parents received the news, they called Grampa, asking why he did such a thing. His response? "I need my grandson and you a lot more than I need the thousand dollars. I made a mistake. It was my responsibility to fix it."

I wonder if I would have solved the problem this way. Would you? The solution Grampa Mullins chose won't work for everyone, but it brought this family back together again.

Grandparents like Grampa Mullins sometimes make mistakes because they think of their adult children as the kids they once were and themselves as still the authority figure in their children's lives. This can cause problems, as you're about to see.

Relating to Children as Adults

It's hard for some grandparents to relinquish authority to a "child" with a family of his or her own. Sharon was a twenty-year-old mother who went back to work immediately after her baby was born. Sharon's mother, Helen, provided day-care for

Timmy in her home. As time went by, it became increasingly difficult for Sharon to pry Timmy away from his grandmother, who adored him and cared for him as if he were her own.

This grandmother took her job too seriously, telling Sharon at the end of the day what to feed the child for dinner and precisely when to put him to bed, leaving her stressed-out daughter competing with her own mother for the attention and affection of her child. "He cries for his Grandma at bath time," Sharon said. "He doesn't settle down until I put him to bed. Then we start all over again the next day."

It's not easy to be a full-time babysitter *and* grandmother, then switch over to *just* grandmother in an advisory role at the end of the day. It takes daily reinforcement of the mother's relationship with the child, talking about her, creating things for her, making the mother a very real part of the child's day until she comes for him. Emotional grandmothers can have a hard time with this, but we must remember to stay in the grandparent role. Talk to the parent. Say something like "You know how much I love Timmy, but maybe I love him too much. Can we talk about it?"

Honest communication is vital to honoring your child's position as parent and acknowledging that your *grandchild* is not your *child*. God gives grace to godly grandparents to deal with such sticky circumstances before a problem arises.

COMMUNICATING WITH THE GATEKEEPER

The great majority of family squabbles come from lack of communication or unclear communication, and that's certainly true in grandparenting. Example: Grandma allows Susie to watch television when she visits, but television is taboo at Susie's house. Grandma's in trouble. It's easy to see that Susie's mother and Grandma, at the very least, are not communicating clearly. This kind of oversight can lead to hurt feelings and distrust.

Clear communication is one of God's instruments of grace that allows grandparents to partner with parents in raising godly children.

- ❖ *Asking questions,* helps us avoid the risk of losing our influence in our grandchildren's lives.
- ❖ *Asking permission* when we are not sure protects the authority of the parent and our role as grandparent.

One of the toughest conversations to have with an adult child is one where you set boundaries. Whether they know it or not, your grandchildren's parents can "dump on you"—a term not unique to nineties grandparents, and one I hear far too often.

"My daughter thinks I am a built-in babysitter at no charge! Aren't I entitled to a life of my own?" That is being "dumped on." And grandparents shouldn't have to take it. The best resolution I've heard for this serious problem came from a dear Texas grandmother who told me this story:

> I love my daughter, and I am good friends with her husband. They have given us three of the best little grand-kids you'd ever want. Darlene took a part-time job, four hours a day, three days a week; and I was glad to take the children. Then her job went to full-time and I still had the kids, sometimes until after six and for dinner. I began praying about it.
>
> One morning when she dropped the kids off, I told her I wanted to talk to her that night. She came early, wondering what I wanted. I told her that from then on I would be happy to take the children three days a week, but that on Mondays I would be going to circle meeting and that I wanted to keep Fridays free to go on short trips with Grandpa. I also told her that since she was earning a good salary, I would expect to be paid two hundred dollars per month for my services.

It was the hardest thing I've ever done. My heart was in my throat, but I had to do it for my own sanity. Darlene took it just fine. She hugged me and told me she was sorry for not realizing how she had imposed on me. She contracted with a day-care center close to her work, and last month the kids started going there full time.

Resolving Conflicts

Darlene's mother exhibited the courage to communicate what is required for resolution of family problems. In his book, *Between Parents and Grandparents,* renowned researcher of grandparent issues Dr. Arthur Kornhaber offers these ten steps to take in family conflicts:

1. Assess the situation. What has happened?
2. What is the status of the problem? Is it just beginning or at the boiling point?
3. What are the attitudes of those involved in the problem? Am I at fault? Does someone think I am, and I'm not? Could I do something to make it better?
4. Talk to other family members and get their opinions. Try to understand everyone's point of view by pretending you are an attorney defending *their* case.
5. Analyze the components of the problem and what caused it. Are the problems caused by different lifestyles, personalities, or attitudes?
6. Define the common interests of the parties.
7. Using common interests, think about helpful options for working out the existing problem.
8. Formulate a plan using common interests and best options.
9. Communicate your plan directly to the party or parties involved. Discuss your plan as a starting point to a working plan all parties will agree to honor.

10. Carry out the plan. Monitor, discuss, and improve the plan when necessary.[1]

Grown children who are upset or even antagonistic toward their parents over some situation are still the gatekeepers of the grandchildren. Personal conflict between grandparent and parents cannot be ignored. It will fester and grow out of proportion to the actual circumstance. It cannot be attacked with accusatory statements that inflame and provoke. It must be dealt with quickly, prayerfully, and in Christian love if grandparents expect to have an ongoing relationship with their grandchildren. Of course, the best solution to conflict is to take the initiative to stop it before it starts.

PREVENTING CONFLICT WITH PARENTS

Adeline told everyone but her daughter-in-law, Karen, about her feelings. She told her neighbor about how she disapproved of the "plug" the children put in her grandbaby's mouth to keep her quiet. She told her sisters about how awful it was that the couple had gone on a weekend trip and left the baby with Karen's parents. She told everybody everything. Finally some of what she said got back to Karen, causing hard feelings. As a result, the gate was less open to the grandchild.

This kind of standoff will continue until one party goes to the other all prayed up and covered with God's grace to say, "Something's wrong here. Let's fix it."

Here are some things a grandparent can do that will prevent conflict and keep the parent/grandparent relationship running smoothly:

1. Appreciate their position as parents. Remember your own parenting years—the stress, disappointments, unexpected emergencies, sick kids, weariness.
2. Respect them for the good job they are doing, not the job you *wish* they were doing.

3. Support them tangibly and intangibly while keeping their dignity and authority intact.

4. Establish acceptable boundaries for your time, energy, and your cost of doing business as a grandparent.

5. Listen twice as much as you talk. A careful listener will hear between the lines and know what to do or what not to do.

6. Watch for body language. Parents who can't find the words to say what they are thinking may show it by the way they sit, stand, move, or pay attention to you.

7. Confront with love before the problem begins. "This is the way I've always done it, dear. You'll have to tell me if it's not right."

8. Encourage, pray for, and honor the parent every day. Speaking positively about the parent personally and to others enhances a pattern of open and loving communication.

GRACE PRINCIPLE:

God's grace is evident in children and grandchildren.

Children's children are a crown to the aged,
and parents are the pride of their children.

— Proverbs 17:6

Another way to partner with parents is to help them and your grandchildren learn how to be good stewards of the earthly treasure temporarily entrusted to us by our gracious God.

ॐ

Chapter 4

GRANDPARENTS AND MONEY

Good old Mom gave her divorced son fifty dollars or so every time he was in a bind and couldn't make it through the week, not realizing that she was enabling her son to fail and was robbing him of his chance to succeed on his own.

Another grandmother and her husband made substantial loans to their married daughter so that the young family of four could have a house instead of living in an apartment—loans to be repaid when the kids could afford it. But when it came time for the money to be repaid, the kids still couldn't afford it. Four years later, they still can't afford it, and the grandparents need their money back.

Paul teaches in 1 Timothy 5:8, "If anyone does not provide for his relatives, and especially for his immediate family, he has denied the faith and is worse than an unbeliever." How much do we give of our earthly treasure to our children for the well-being of our grandchildren? Do we give freely or do we expect to get it back? When should we give? When should we not? What is our responsibility?

In his book, *Living the Responsible Life*, Cecil A. Ray, director of the Stewardship Division, Baptist General Convention of Texas, reminds us what living the responsible life of a Christian steward involves:

1. Recognizing God as the creator and designer of all things.
2. Acknowledging that God is the owner and that we are trust-holders and managers.
3. Seeking to understand God's plan for His world and our role as the trusted representatives of God in the use and management of all creation.
4. Accepting Christ as the Lord of life and committing ourselves to honor Him in all relationships to and use of material things.
5. Adopting a God-honoring lifestyle in the acquiring or earning of material possessions, the managing of all material possessions, and the giving of both self and possessions in service to Christ.[1]

Remembering these responsibilities when addressing monetary decisions relating to our children and their children, the Christian grandparent will:

Pray. Whether the need is expressed to you or you observe it yourself, pray before taking action. God may want to do something else in the situation. Take time to discern His will and consider alternatives.

Plan. Grandparents should have a written financial plan including projected income and expenses for the next twelve months. God's Word makes it clear that we are to plan. Planning brings balance and responsibility into our lives and sets a good example for children and grandchildren.

Partner. Our children and their children are their own family unit. We don't want to undermine the parents' authority by failing to consult with them about our financial plans for our grandchildren. Of course, we're not talking about small amounts of money grandparents might dole out from time to time. But when the amounts are significant, we need to partner with parents.

Grandparents must be willing to clearly communicate intentions *and* expectations in financial transactions even at the risk of jeopardizing the relationships with their children and grandchildren.

Dave Bragonier is an area coordinator for Larry Burkett's Christian Financial Concepts and director of Barnabus, Inc., a Christian financial training ministry. He offers five reasons grandparents might want to avoid gift-giving at a particular time:

1. If your motivation is guilt about something that happened or didn't happen in the past.
2. If the gift-giving process doesn't teach the child something about God and biblical principles.
3. If the child is outwardly rebellious against God. (Unless your gift might be an instrument to draw him or her to eternal salvation.)
4. If you don't have it to give. We don't always have to be the "dollar." We can be the "process" toward fulfillment of the goal.
5. If you are indulging them. As grandparents, we must be willing to allow our children and grandchildren to suffer in order for God to bring about the changes He wants in their lives.[2]

GIFTING

Some grandparents receive great satisfaction from watching the progress a grandchild makes because of their gift. Others prefer to trust the money to a third party, a trustee who monitors changes in the child's life. Others wish to name the grandchildren in a will.

Creative grandparents come up with clever ways to give of their earthly treasure. One took a photograph of an heirloom, then sold it and gave the money and the photo to a grandchild when that child turned eighteen.

Another had a special party at her home for three grand-daughters at which she instructed the girls to go through her jewelry and some other valuable items and select the items they each would like to have willed to them. The grandmother left the house while the girls did as she asked. When she returned an hour later, Grandmother marked each item to be willed to each granddaughter, and that was that.

God's Word in 1 Timothy 6:7 reminds us that "We brought nothing into the world, and we can take nothing out of it." Assigning what the Lord has temporarily entrusted to us before or after our death is a personal decision.

Financial planners offer a wide variety of good ideas for grandparent consideration. One is called a giftrust which allows a grandparent to provide a much larger financial contribution to a grandchild's future than they can afford in one lump sum today. An initial gift of $250 or more is placed in an irrevocable trust for a minimum of ten years or until the beneficiary reaches the age of majority, whichever is more. During the term of the trust, the original money and any income it earns are invested and reinvested. The child watches it grow yearly as he or she receives annual statements.

An endearing feature of the giftrust is a personal inscription from the giver that appears on each statement so that even after the grandparent has died, the child is reminded of the one who gave the gift.

Another more complex type of irrevocable trust is the Generation Skipping Trust (GST). Its key feature is that assets of the trust do not pass directly to the usual heirs, i.e., the children, but skip a generation and pass to the grandchildren. Children may or may not receive income from this trust but do not control the assets. The advantage of the GST is that it avoids one level of estate taxes, which for some can be substantial. The GST is harder to do and has restrictions, but properly planned, it can be leveraged into a sizable trust for the benefit of multiple generations.[4]

Whatever your decision regarding gifting for the future, providing college funds, or buying that first car for a grandchild, before you make it, ask yourself:

1. Will this gift have a positive or negative influence on the child's incentive to make his or her own way in the world?
2. Am I creating an expectation that he or she needn't have to be resourceful? That Grandma or Grandpa will bail them out of such trouble as paying traffic tickets or overdue rent?
3. As I give this gift or loan, am I investing in the temporal or the eternal welfare of this grandchild?
4. What are the tax consequences to giving this gift?

HELPING TO EDUCATE YOUR GRANDCHILD

Grandparents want to see grandchildren reach their full potential. That might mean going on to higher education which can be an expensive proposition these days. A grandparent can serve in an advisory role to a parent, investigating the many and varied fee programs and other schooling opportunities available to students. Tuition and other costs are different in different parts of the country. Tuition, room, and board at one school may be $18-$20,000 per year and at another $12-$14,000. Researching schools can be time-consuming, and busy parents and students might welcome a partner in the work.

Grandparents may want to contribute financially to a grandchild's education.

Creative planning and funding options are available to increase savings for the higher education of a grandchild. Ask of a financial planner about the advantages of employing grandchildren in your business, tuition prepayment plans, and ways in which a life insurance policy can be used as a savings program. Other creative funding options include traditional savings programs such as treasury bills, certificates of deposit (CDs), and money market accounts. Although these savings programs are safe and investors usually have access to money with little or no penalties, interest rates may fluctuate dramatically over time. Lower rates would require additional savings to meet future expenses.[5]

FINANCIAL PARTNERING

Grandparents can encourage parents from before the day a grandchild is born to plan for the child's financial future, even by offering to match dollars to help the fund grow. For example, if parents and grandparents each contributed $50 for a total of $100 each month at 6 percent compounded interest for eighteen years, that amount would grow to $38,929!

Matching earned dollars with a young grandchild is a good incentive for them to save as well. Kids can surprise you when it comes to saving money. I remember when Grandpa Endicott educated our nine-year-old grandson, Jeremy, about the virtues of saving by helping him open an account with his own passbook. Grandpa promised to match every dollar Jeremy could put in the account. At the end of two short months, Jeremy notified his grandfather that he owed him $43.

Partnering with a grown grandchild to purchase a first house is another way of teaching financial responsibility while helping make the dream of "a home of their own" come true. There's a new financial idea that can satisfy the goals of both the grandparents and the children's by allowing the grandchildren to maintain their independence and the grandparents to keep their net worth.

The concept is called a shared equity financing arrangement or SEFA. It uses the combined resources of grandparents and grandchildren. Under SEFA, the grandparents usually pay the down payment and closing costs. The grandchildren commit to pay some or all of the monthly carrying costs. In exchange for meeting their respective obligations, the parties to the agreement share ownershp of the house—the grandparents as owner/investors and the grandchildren as owner/occupants.

There are tax and investment benefits all around when the arrangement is handled responsibly. SEFA is complicated but "do-able." Ask a certified public account or a financial planner about SEFA as a potential way to help grandchildren step into the American dream without overstepping your own finances.[6]

Financial partnering with grandchildren is a tangible way to say, "I trust you. I believe in you." In Ephesians 5:15–16, Paul admonishes us to buy up the time in these days of rampant evil, missing no opportunity to teach and witness. If grandparents are alert, they have many opportunities to teach grandchildren about money. By demonstrating the fundamentals of financial responsibility, grandparents can give grandchildren an early understanding of stewardship.

GIVING TO THE CHURCH

For the committed Christian, giving to the church is not an option; it is a privilege. It is an act of worship. The Bible says that the steward is to give the first fruits, proportionately and systematically, to the church. The attitude of the giver and the manner of giving are as important as the mechanics. The gift should be both an act of thanksgiving and a way of dedicating one's total self to God.

Richard B. Cunningham writes in *Resource Unlimited:*

> The Christian gives to various good causes. There are quite different occasions and ways to give to the church. At a mimimum, these would include one's systematic and proportionate giving, the giving of wealth and accumu-

lated income, and the giving of estates at the end of one's life. Gifts should be presented at times and in ways that best achieve biblical purposes of giving and high standards of stewardship."[7]

Enough Money to Retire

My husband finally retired one year ago at age sixty-six. Oh, to hear him tell it, this was going to be the best time of our lives. He could fish, and I could write. We live on Puget Sound near Seattle; and he does fish, and I write. But I cannot tell you it has been easy for Bill. You see, underneath the facade of his delight in retirement is the strong work ethic of a man whose alarm clock, for forty-five years, told him to rise at 5:00 A.M. and go someplace where he was expected to work.

Bill has many interests to occupy his time at home in retirement. After all, we do have twelve perfect grandchildren. He is editor of the *33rd Division Newsletter,* a national news-letter for fellow comrades who served in the Pacific during World War II. Bill also enjoys woodworking in his shop or clearing land and developing property. But he isn't going someplace, the same place, every weekday. He isn't reporting in. That difference is still, even after a year, hard to deal with.

It's different for me, too, having him around more of the time. But Bill and I are good friends. We work together, talking out our dreams and making them come true. We can disagree, even argue, and stay friends because of our commitment to each other and our shared faith.

We talked a lot about his retirement. We took a number of years to work up to it psychologically. We could do that part. But in order to be ready for retirement *financially,* we had to consult the experts. Here is some information that motivated us to plan financially for retirement, taken from a survey published in *Money* magazine in 1991 and reported by Barbara Deane in her book, *Getting Ready for a Great Retirement:*

❖ twenty-three percent of those over fifty-five said they are not financially able to retire, up seven points in one year.

❖ ninety-three percent voiced concern about health care costs, also up seven points in one year.

❖ eighty-five percent are afraid that nursing home costs could ruin them or their families financially.

❖ ninety percent think that at some future time they will need financial help from their children or from the government, up from 79 percent the year before.

❖ eighty-three percent are afraid that their income will not meet their needs in the future, up from 74 percent in the previous year.[8]

Here are a few tips to help you along the way:

❖ Choose a financial planner as carefully as you would a physician or an attorney.

❖ Estimate your projected living costs. Create a plan that covers all aspects of your life.

❖ Seriously consider buying a Medigap insurance policy, but be careful to ignore the advertising and choose the one that fits your needs.

❖ Stay informed. Information on medical insurance coverage, investments, and taxation is outdated very quickly.

❖ It's never too early or too late to plan for retirement. Do it with a professional advisor you trust.

Planning to Survive

Can one really *plan* to survive the death of a spouse? Well, certainly not emotionally. Many grandparents have told me that even after a mate's long illness, the event of death is always difficult to bear. But there are some practical steps both of you can take now which might make such an event just a little easier to bear and preserve the survivor's future.

Widows fifty-five and older still outnumber widowers about seven to one. Lawyers and financial counselors say that their saddest interviews are with older women who were financially unprepared for widowhood. Many sail through the parenting season, through mid-life, and into old age completely dependent upon their husbands. For whatever reason, they are ill-prepared to lead a life alone.

A good plan, however, benefits a husband as well as a wife. Attorney Lyle K. Wilson suggests these important points:

1. *Husband and wife should sit down together early to discuss financial arrangements for retirement.* The younger you are, the less long-term care or life insurance costs. Such a conversation can be emotional, but you need to do it.

2. *Create a will or living trust arrangement that provides for orderly disposition of the estate.* This is foundational and should be a priority, even for young couples. Without a plan, disposition will be different from what was intended. In one case, a couple in a second marriage was living in a home owned by the wife before the marriage. She died without a will, and under the laws of that state, her children from the first marriage were entitled to half of her estate, including the house. Instead of her husband staying on in the house, it had to be sold and the funds divided, which caused a great deal of anger between the stepchildren and the widower. Do not use a mail-order form for an important document such as a will or living trust. See a competent, experienced attorney.

3. *Update the will or living trust as changes occur.*

4. *Be familiar with all bank accounts, bank locations, account numbers, and balances.* If possible, write down the name of a contact at each financial institution.

5. *Understand all stock certificates and bonds owned.*

6. *Know your insurance agent's name and telephone number* plus the amounts and stipulations of each policy.

7. *Consider having a living will/directive to physicians/durable power of attorney.* These inexpensive documents can save a lot of problems. Again, obtain the services of a competent attorney to help you. One woman went to a bookstore for what she thought was a form for durable power of attorney. It was in reality a "special" durable power of attorney with a big blank space in the middle to be filled out with specifics. The husband and wife signed the form, even had it notarized without filling out the specifics in the blank space. It said nothing and was invalid. Bookstore forms may not cover what needs to be covered. If you buy one, take it to an attorney.

8. *Make funeral arrangements ahead of time,* especially if you have special desires.

9. *Keep all important papers in one easily accessible place.*

10. *Do not presume you will go first.* You may never see tour buses loaded with older men, but we can't presuppose that the wife will survive the husband or vice versa. Never plan around one or the other. Take care of both of you!

GRACE PRINCIPLE:

We cannot earn God's grace.

He saved us, not because of deeds done by us in righteousness, but in virtue of his own mercy, by the washing of regeneration and renewal in the Holy Spirit, which he poured out upon us richly through Jesus Christ our Savior, so that we might be justified by his grace and become heirs in hope of eternal life.

— Titus 3:5–7, RSV

Teaching grandchildren by strengthening their faith as they learn about their world and themselves is an awesome responsibility examined next in part 2.

ॐ

HELPING
GRANDCHILDREN GROW

Children have a sixth sense about right and wrong, truth and lies, and who really loves them.

Grandparents know that somehow. Because we are not the primary authority figure in a grandchild's life, we have a unique place in the family. We can teach principles and values in a non-threatening way because we are not in control. We can help them grow according to God's plan.

Let my teaching fall like rain
and my words descend like dew,
like showers on new grass,
like abundant rain on tender plants.
I will proclaim the name of the Lord.
Oh, praise the greatness of our God!

— Deuteronomy 32:2–3

Chapter 5

GRANDPARENTS AS TEACHERS

Let the little children come unto me" (Matt. 19:14). God's desire is that every child know Him as heavenly Father, Jesus as Savior, and the Holy Spirit as their indwelling guide as they grow. Grandparents can be one of God's instruments of grace in this effort when we adopt a prayerful approach to teaching these and other truths.

Instilling Christian principles and values in grandchildren today can be a daunting task. But we fight the good fight. We continue to live the Christian life, talk the Christian life, love the Christian life. We teach by example and pray our grandchildren will be reinforced in their faith.

STRENGTHENING THEIR FAITH

We must always realize that our grandchildren are constantly growing and changing. We should also be aware that the things that we teach and the methods we use to teach those things must reflect the needs of our grandchildren at their current stage of development. Christian grandparents must be aware of what it is that God wants our grandchildren to know as they grow.

	What Is Happening in Their Lives?	What God Wants Them to Know
Preschool Grandchildren: The Vulnerable Age	Preschoolers do not comprehend Ecclesiastes. They do know hugs, feeling loved, feeling safe, and having fun. They are curious. They're afraid of monsters and being left alone. They ask "Why?" They trust everyone because they want to.	That He is their Heavenly Father. He never leaves them. He is a friend who is always watching over them to keep them and their loved ones safe. That they can talk to God by prayer and He answers. That He is in control of the whole world. God loves them. God will always love them, no matter what happens.
School Age Grandchildren: The Age of Insecurity	Unsure about themselves, their skills, their worth, their future. When they look in the mirror, they wonder who they are, what they can do and should do. They are exploring. Trying their wings. Trying their parents. Pushing boundaries.	That God loves them just the way they are. That they are valuable. He loves them even when they make mistakes. He will never give up on them. That God loves the truth. He is Truth. Others may disappoint them but God never will. They can trust Him. God wants them to obey His teachings. That losing is a part of learning. That He needs fellowship with them.
Teenage Grandchildren: Almost Grown Up	Doubting what they believe. Sexual issues, peer pressure, media influence, rebelliousness, apathy, worry, fast-track schedules, noise. Music and friends have top priority. Teens need encouragement to find answers to questions themselves. Forcefed faith will be rejected.	That God's promises are true. That to be faithful to God is to live an exciting life. That He is still in control in the good times and bad. That they can be a blessing to others. That God is a God of second chances. He loves them unconditionally and will never leave them as they grow to adulthood and responsibility, even when they become grandparents and great-grandparents!

Here is a list of Scripture thoughts to help you help grandchildren understand the love and grace of God during the various stages of growth and change they will experience:

Preschool:

1. I am your heavenly Father who never leaves you.
   — Hebrews 13:5

2. I will keep you safe.
   — Psalm 4:8

3. I hear your prayers.
   — Psalm 138:3; Jeremiah 33:3

4. I control the world.
   — Psalm 33:6–12; Psalm 103:19

5. I love you and will always love you, no matter what happens.
   — Psalm 118:1, 29

School Age:

1. I love you just the way you are; you are valuable.
   — Psalm 139:13–16

2. I always keep My promises.
   — 1 Kings 8:56; Psalm 119:89

3. I love you even when you make mistakes.
   — Psalm 103:8–14

4. I will never give up on you.
   — 2 Timothy 2:13; Hebrews 13:5

5. I love the truth.
   — Exodus 20:16; Ephesians 4:25

6. I am truth.
   — John 14:6

7. I will never disappoint you, even though others may.
   — Psalm 27:10

8. You can trust Me.
   — Psalm 117:2; 2 Thessalonians 3:3

9. I want you to obey My teachings.
   — Deuteronomy 11:1; 26–28; 1 Samuel 20:22; Matthew 5:19; John 15:14

10. Be content in all things.
— Philippians 4:11–13

11. I need fellowship with you.
— Micah 6:8; Revelation 3:20

Teenage:

1. My promises are true.
— 2 Corinthians 1:20

2. Being faithful to Me leads to an exciting life.
— Psalm 34:8–14; Psalm 103:4–5; John 10:10

3. I am in control in good times and bad.
— Genesis 50:19–20; Psalm 25:10

4. You can be a blessing to others.
— Genesis 12:2–3

5. I am the God of second chances.
— John 21:15–19

6. I love you unconditionally.
— Psalm 103:8–14

7. I will never leave you, even as you grow to adulthood.
— Psalm 119:90; Isaiah 46:4

We are in a battle for the souls of our grandchildren. Our most important task is to strengthen their faith in Jesus Christ. My friend Caralee's grandmother and grandfather were wonderful teachers of the faith by the way they lived their lives. They started each day with God's Word. It had been their sure foundation in the past and would be their guiding light for the future. Their final possessions were few, yet they died wealthy. As son and daughter of the King, they owned a storehouse of accomplishments and memories. No book will be written about them, no monuments erected in their honor. But all three of Caralee's sons have made a commitment to Jesus Christ and are part of the living memorial to their grandparents' greatest accomplishment—influencing others for Christ by strengthening their faith in Christ.

GREAT-GRANDPARENTS AS TEACHERS

The family with a great-grandparent or a great-great-grandparent is truly blessed, because they have a living history book who can use a half-century or more of knowledge to influence others for Christ!

One young woman said of her great-grandmother, "Nonnie is our family treasure. We love her so much, and she deserves our love. Her life has not been easy, but her faith in God is unshaken. She has strengthened our faith by her own witness."

I enjoy going to elementary schools to teach creative writing. I always save time for a few questions about grandparents. On one occasion I asked whether anyone in the class had a great-grandparent. A little fellow raised his hand to say, "I have one! I'd rather listen to Pops than watch TV. He tells these really cool stories about the olden days, and he knows just about everything!"

Great-grandparents are symbols of family continuity and character. Kids can learn about the past, family traditions, and their own parents and grandparents just by being around a great-grandparent. Active, involved great-grandparents model graceful longevity for the whole family. And longevity is our future! Over 40 percent of older people live long enough to become great-grandparents. In the near future, there will be many great-grandparents, living longer, healthier lives.

If you are one who has graduated to great-grandparenting, *congratulations!* I hope you are blessed with the energy and vitality to take your royal title to new and greater heights!

TEACHING BY ENCOURAGING

Johnny quit the basketball team after two seasons on the bench. He told his grandfather he was tired of being called "Shorty" and never getting a chance to play. He said, "What's the use? I'm just no good. Besides, they'll never miss me."

Johnny's grandfather encouraged him to try again, telling him that he had his two best friends rooting for him—his grandfather and Jesus. The boy had another season on the bench, but he knew he wasn't a quitter. His grandfather attended every game. Johnny's teammates gradually noticed his attitude change, and their ridicule turned to respect. Johnny learned a lesson about not giving up that perhaps no one but his grandfather could have taught him. His grandfather had been a safe place to take his fears, his hurt, and his confusion. He gave Johnny the courage to begin again.

It's a cruel world out there. Even a healthy, well-adjusted child can feel inferior or insecure at times. There can be many reasons children think they don't measure up. Low self-esteem can show up at any age. Grandparents who partner with parents to rebuild the fragile self-confidence and self-worth of a grandchild are following God's plan for that child.

Here are some sources of low self-esteem in children. If one or two are familiar, look into God's plan regarding that issue.

Source	_God's Plan_
Peer Pressure	Matthew 6:25

"I'm not good enough."
"Everybody's doing it."

Worry About Appearance	1 Samuel 16:7

"I always look weird!"
"I hate my nose!"

Mistakes	Isaiah 43:1-7

"I can't do anything right!"
"I can never fix it."

Critical Parents	Exodus 20:12

"I'll never be able to please them."
"My parents don't love me."

Fear	Isaiah 41:10

"I can't do it."
"I'm afraid to try."

Caution: Depression is far more serious than low self-esteem. Ask your doctor for information on the differences. If your grandchild exhibits a chronic behavior pattern of depression, talk to the parents. Urge them to get professional help for your grandchild. The suicide rate among adolescents has climbed steadily over the last thirty years and is now the second leading cause of death among teens. The leading cause is auto accidents, and experts speculate that many single-car accidents are intentional suicide by depressed youth. (In your devotion time, read the Book of Jonah for an understanding of his struggle with depression.)

TEACHING RESPECT FOR PEOPLE AND PROPERTY

Kids have their own problems with control and power. It isn't enough that a child's hormones are raging during the teen years, but we also have a society that condones and even encourages sex and violence! Many nineties parents struggle with their child's disrespect for values, for other people, and for things.

Grandparents can help. Even though we are not the primary authority figure in a grandchild's life, we can support parents by being informed of current trends and helping temper a grandchild's rebellious spirit when we get a chance.

The key to effective intervention from a grandparent is to counsel as an ally and not as an adversary. That probably won't happen unless a grandchild/grandparent relationship based on mutual trust and respect has been built over time.

WINNING AND LOSING

At the end of a game played with a grandchild, a grandparent has a blessed opportunity to teach principles which could leave a lasting imprint: how to be a gracious winner and how to be a good loser. Have you ever heard either of these remarks from a grandchild after playing a game?

"Ha! Ha! I beat you!"

"I wanted to win! You cheated! I'm not going to play anymore!"

How did you respond? Did you laugh it off, or did you seize the opportunity to teach?

I have been faced with that opportunity many times while playing Old Maid or rummy or a board game with my grandchildren. Years ago, I instituted a rule that must be followed or "Grandma won't play." The rule is that the loser of a game always congratulates the winner and shakes the winner's hand. Oh, boy! Sometimes that is hard to do, but we do not resume play until that gesture is made. I'm glad to tell you that prompting is no longer needed with any of my grandchildren, even Gabrielle, who is four. When I lose, I immediately offer my hand in congratulations. When I win, I sometimes have to wait, but she doesn't let me down. Out comes her little hand and, although reluctantly, she says the word, then breaks out in that irresistible smile.

ANSWERING THEIR QUESTIONS

Who? What? Why? Where? When? The questions of little ones! God's plan is that grandparents answer the easy and the tough questions with patience.

On a plane trip, I sat next to a grandparent and her granddaughter, who was about three years old. Passengers were buckling up for a long flight. As we waited to take off, the little girl asked in a high-pitched, anxious voice, "Why aren't we going yet? What is that over there? Who's that lady? When do we get there? Why aren't we going yet? Why? Why? Why?"

The patient grandmother responded to the relentless questioning in a low, gentle tone. "We'll take off soon. That's the baggage truck. That lady is going to travel with us. Soon, dear. Pretty soon, dear. The pilot isn't quite ready yet."

"Why?" the child persisted.

Passengers around us grimaced at the child's loud questioning. I smiled and silently congratulated the grandmother for her patience with a stage of growth common to all children, a stage to be cherished, for it is all too quickly gone.

As a grandchild grows, the questions become more and more serious and more and more important. Some answers can make the difference in their good health, their safety, or their salvation. All of a grandchild's questions at any age deserve to be answered with patience, wisdom, honesty, and consistency.

TEACHING BY LISTENING

"Mom and Dad are so busy. I'm glad I have my grandparents to listen to me about what's going on. I love to talk to them, because I know they're really listening."

In this microwave, hurry-up society, let us be faithful listeners, ports in the storm, nonjudgmental shoulders in times of trouble or sorrow, wise counselors who solve problems by listening, allowing a grandchild to come to his or her own conclusions. God gave us one mouth and two ears. Might that mean that we are supposed to listen twice as much as we talk?

Marilyn's granddaughter calls her often. Amanda, now sixteen, loves animals, so the calls are usually something like "I just couldn't leave this stray cat out in the cold. Should I keep it?" Or, "Grandma! This dog was hit by a car and is bleeding and everything! I'm going to take it to the vet. How am I going to pay for it?"

Marilyn always listens. Then she asks pertinent questions such as, "Don't you already have a cat?" Or, "How much do you have in your savings account?" Amanda comes to her own conclusions and makes her own judgments about situations after talking with a grandmother who patiently helps her sort things out.

Teaching Individually

Every child is unique before God. Some grandparents have a tendency to lump the grandkids together like oranges or bananas. When this happens, grandparents can miss the target on grandchildren's likes and dislikes and end up with hurt feelings and unhappy kids. These grandparents also miss out on the remarkable individuality of every child. What a joy it is to watch each grandchild learn and grow in his own unique way, and in his own time.

Look at each one as Jesus sees each child, precious in His sight.

Avoid Negative Teaching

Tom was fifteen years old when his paternal grandfather died. Grandpa Harvey was an alcoholic who abused the power of the tongue and the people nearest and dearest to him. At his grandfather's funeral service, Tom said, "I learned a lot from Grandpa. I learned how not to live."

What a sad legacy! All that was good about the grandparent/grandchild relationship had been overshadowed by destructive habits.

In 1 Corinthians 11:1 (NASB), Paul said, "Be imitators of me, just as I also am of Christ." Besides displaying bad habits such as drinking, smoking, arguing and swearing, before grandchildren, here are three key areas to avoid:

- ❖ *Prejudice*—a negative prejudgment of another person solely based on such external factors as a difference in race, social status, financial condition, or outward appearance (clothes, hair, makeup, etc.).
- ❖ *Gossip*—telling stories (true or untrue) about other people for your personal enjoyment or profit.

❖ *Self-centeredness*—trying to arrange everything in life to bring personal peace and comfort to you no matter what it causes in others' lives.

Children imitate those they love the most. Everything we do and say around a grandchild risks mimmicking. Grandchildren are waiting for an opportunity to act just like us, as in this example from one grandson: "Why are you going to wash my mouth out with soap, Grandma? That's the same word Grandpa said when he hit his finger!"

GRACE PRINCIPLE:

God's grace brings responsibility.

As each one has received a special gift, employ it in serving one another, as good stewards of the manifold grace of God.

— 1 Peter 4:10, NASB

We look now to healthy, positive ways to use our grandparent gifts of grace in matters of discipline.

℃

Chapter 6

DISCIPLINING GRANDCHILDREN

Y ou are visiting your daughter-in-law and your two-year-old granddaughter at their home. When your daughter-in-law leaves the room for a moment, your granddaughter looks you squarely in the eye and reaches for the latch of the cabinet her mother just told her not to touch. What do you do?

You are at your home baby-sitting your two-year-old granddaughter. Your granddaughter looks you squarely in the eye and reaches for the latch of the cabinet you just told her not to touch. What do you do?

In both instances, you *defer to the parents.* In the first scenario, immediately call the incident to your daughter-in-law's attention and let her do the disciplining. In the second instance, at your home, follow through with whatever discipline for such an incident they have prescribed.

"What should I do if . . . ?" is one of the most important questions a babysitting grandparent will ask a parent. We must get our disciplinary orders from the parent. *Discipline of a grandchild is not grandparent business.* Ask the parent(s) what they expect when discipline is necessary. What is the child accustomed to? Time out? A spank on the hand? Play restriction? A nap? And that's what you do when you're in charge.

Of course, there are exceptions to that rule: when a child repeatedly disobeys or is completly unruly to the extent of damaging property or endangering themselves or someone else. But, generally, discipline is the province of the parent(s), and partnering with them on this subject is very important.

"Oppositional children" come in all sizes. In his book on behavior problems, *Kid Think*, Dr. William Lee Carter says:

- ❖ An eighteen-month-old may look his parent squarely in the eye as he opens a forbidden cabinet door.
- ❖ A six-year-old may jeer and taunt her mother immediately following a tantrum.
- ❖ An eight-year-old may refuse to come into the house when he hears his name called—for the third time.
- ❖ A thirteen-year-old girl may shout "I hate you!" when told that she has applied a bit too much makeup.
- ❖ A high school student may stay out two hours past curfew, knowing his father will be waiting when he gets home.[1]

Thankfully, such challenges to authority are usually short-lived and are just a part of growing up. Our job is to survive these stages, but that sometimes requires a great deal of grand-parenting maturity and faith.

Also, societal rules have changed. For example, light physical punishment such as spanking that was doled out in our parenting season might be labeled "abuse" today.

Here is a list of possible discipline problems that may confront a grandparent. Think about how you would handle each one, and then take time to look up the Scripture and read God's plan for each circumstance:

Problem	God's Plan
Lying	Exodus 20:16
Swearing	Matthew 5:34–36
Cheating	Leviticus 19:35–36
Tantrums	Proverbs 16:32

Stealing .... Exodus 20:15

Fighting .... Galatians 5:19–21

Disobedience.......................... Proverbs 6:20

Pouting .... Ephesians 4:26

LACK OF DISCIPLINE

Observing the lack of parental discipline of a grandchild can make a grandparent's blood pressure rise. We might think, *A dose of discipline would do that child a lot of good!*

Doris felt that way. She and her daughter, Jenny, are good friends and spend a lot of time together accompanied by grandson Matt, age nine. Doris was often bothered by the way Jenny let Matt "get away with murder." One day at the mall, Doris observed Jenny giving Matt anything he wanted. He begged his mother to buy him a sweatshirt Doris thought far too expensive. He got it. Matt had a tantrum in front of the movie theater, so he got to see the movie he wanted to see. During the movie he made several trips to the candy and popcorn counter. After the movie Mom gave Matt quarters for the video machines. Sitting through that was the last straw for Grandma. In the car coming home from the mall, Doris let her daughter have it right in front of Matt. "How can you let him get away with that? Do you realize how he manipulates you to get anything he wants? This child needs discipline!"

Jenny didn't take that well at all. She was seething. The rest of the trip home was silent. When they arrived at the house, Jenny and Matt got out, Jenny slammed the car door, and Doris drove away.

It wasn't that Doris thought Jenny was a bad mother. On the contrary, she admired almost all of her mothering techniques. Grandma had just observed enough spoiling, and the emotions she had stuffed for years came out all at once. Stored feelings are like a time bomb ready to explode. Grandma made a mistake by making "you" statements rather than "I" statements such as "I'm concerned" or "I wonder if Matt realizes how blessed he is." Gentle grandparent talk like that takes the sting out of statements, even though a grandparent might feel strongly about the situation. Attacking instead of confronting with love will set the bomb off every time.

Doris told me, "It took almost a year for us to get over that incident and apologize to each other."

Too Much Discipline

On the other hand, a grandparent might think a parent is too tough on a child: *I never disciplined him that way when he was little! Why is he so strict on his own child?*

We would like to intervene, but we can't. I've heard many, many sad stories from grandmothers, in particular, who have said or done the wrong thing by stepping into the middle of parent/child discipline situations. We're on the sidelines. We do not know all of the intimacies of the parent/child relationship in that household. A case in point was the story one grandmother told of coming to take her daughter and her grandson to lunch.

Just as the happy grandmother stepped into the kitchen, her daughter let go with a verbal barrage that continued for what seemed to Grandma like an eternity—all of it directed at her precious two-year-old grandson who was cowering in the corner. The mother's outburst finally ended with several sharp swats to the boy's bottom before she let him go. Screaming and crying, the child ran toward his room. Grandma intercepted him, sweeping him up into her arms. "Now there, there, sweetie. You poor darling! It's all right. Your grandma loves you."

The daughter was incensed. Her face was red. "I don't believe it! Mother, put him down! Don't you dare try to undo everything I've tried to teach him this week! Yesterday, he flushed three of the aquarium fish down the toilet. This is the second time this week he's mixed the flour in the flour bin with the sugar in the sugar bin. I don't care if you love him! I want him to obey!"

We may see only the end result of a situation and jump to conclusions about what has gone before. Jumping in to "fix it" will incur the parent's wrath and confuse the child. Most importantly, grandparents who step in without being asked undermine the parent's credibility and authority in the eyes of the child.

IT'S NOT OUR JOB

Last fall, I was in the small grocery store near our home. In front of me at the counter were a father and his daughter. She was about seven, barefoot in November, her feet filthy, her print dress tattered and worn, and her long hair was straggly and thick with grime. The girl had dropped several gum packages in the aisle of the store. Her father, also poorly groomed, held on so tight to the little girl's frail-looking arm that she had big tears in her eyes from the squeezing. He was reprimanding her between clenched teeth, "You git in this line and don't you say nothin' smart or I'll paddle you right here and now!"

The child looked up at me and, oh, I wanted to do something! But I knew I couldn't. It's the same with our grandchildren in matters of discipline. We want to do something, but we know we can't. It's simply not our responsibility. Hopefully, we taught our children well enough during our parenting years that as grandparents we won't have to intervene.

Of course, there are times when it is correct, even necessary, to intervene. For example, if a grandparent has knowledge of or suspects that physical or sexual abuse is being perpetrated on a grandchild, that grandparent has not only the right to intervene but the responsibility to act upon that knowledge or suspicion.

Call the National Child Abuse Hotline at 1-800-422-4453 twenty-four hours a day for confidential instructions on how to proceed.

ANSWERING A PARENT'S CALL TO HELP

A wise grandparent will help parents in teaching the discipline lessons some children must learn. This is what happened in the case of a single mother who called on Grandpa in desperation after yet another incident with fourteen-year-old son, Jimmy: "Dad, it's the third time this month I've had to discipline Jimmy. He missed curfew again. He's mad at me. I'm so upset! He's out behind the house pulling weeds on the slope. I told him to work up there for one hour. I'm running out of ideas! Would you talk to him?"

So Grandpa climbed the steep slope and perched on a big rock. There he sat for the remainder of the boy's sentence, he watched his grandson pull weeds and slam them into a big black bag. He listened to a teenager complain about the fact that life isn't fair.

"Every time I do some teeny tiny thing, Mom puts me up here pickin' weeds! I hate it! It's not fair! I was only a half hour late getting home from the ballgame! What's the big deal, anyway?"

On and on the boy complained. His mother peeked out the kitchen window as grandfather and grandson talked until the hour was up. When the twosome walked through the back door into the kitchen, Jimmy fairly ran over to his mother, planted a kiss on her cheek, yelled, "See ya' later, Grandpa!" and sprinted upstairs to his room.

Stunned, Jimmy's mother asked, "What did you do to him?" Grandpa answered, "Oh, I just told him what a special boy he is and how much he means to all of us."

A godly grandparent can help a teenager blossom on the character-building slopes of life.

DISCIPLINING OURSELVES

Like kids, even grandparents can do the darndest things! Some of them we deeply regret. A grandmother in Texas named Audrey told me about having her little granddaughter, Crissy, overnight. It had been a special time of storytelling, hugs, and play. Just watching her sleep, snuggled into her "Crissy bed" had been such a treat!

Now it was Sunday morning, and everything had gone wrong. The alarm clock didn't go off, and they would be late for church. While Audrey prepared a quick breakfast, Crissy spilled cocoa all over the kitchen floor. While Audrey was cleaning that up, Crissy got into Grandma's jewelry case, and broke her favorite necklace. Audrey let the beads lay on the bathroom floor as she scooped up her granddaughter, stood her on the toilet seat, and tried to brush her hair.

Crissy wiggled this way and that. She would not stand still. She wanted a kiss. Then she wanted to get down. Then she did "eensy, weensy spider" on top of her head, messing up her hair. Something snapped in Grandma. Audrey took the little girl by the shoulders and screamed into her face, "Stop acting like a two-year old!"

Crissy was two years old.

The child began to cry. Audrey was mortified by what she had done. Acting her age was exactly what Crissy was doing!

Overtaken by deep regret at losing her temper, it didn't seem all that important to hurry anymore to get to church on time. Audrey cried, too. "Oh, sweetheart, Grandma is so sorry!" She wrapped her arms around her two-year-old granddaughter, and the two of them sank to the floor by the toilet. A half-hour later, they were still there, picking up necklace beads, laughing, and having fun again. Grandma missed church that Sunday, but she learned the importance of self-discipline.

Grandchildren *will indeed* act their age. Part of our responsibility as grandparents is to police our emotions, think ahead, plan ahead, and be prepared to change our plans in mid-stream for the sake of a loving relationship with a cherished grandchild.

GRACE PRINCIPLE:

Grace is God's favor extended to every believer.

Let us therefore draw near with confidence
to the throne of grace, that we may receive mercy
and may find grace to help in time of need.

— Hebrews 4:16, NASB

Some grandparents see through a glass clouded with their own agenda, as we will see in the next chapter.

č

Chapter 7

HEALTHY AND UNHEALTHY CONCERN

Are you concerned about your grandchildren? Do you find yourself in a dilemma about how to express that concern? Have you created strained relationships between your children or grandchildren because you were too zealous in your expressions of concern? Perhaps you are experiencing broken relationships or are struggling with a situation related to something you have seen, heard, or suspected with regard to your children or grandchildren.

Every grandparent can identify with one or more of these circumstances. This chapter helps identify healthy and unhealthy responses to what we see, hear, or suspect that affects our grandchildren. Consider these definitions:

- *Healthy Concern*—an honest, prayer-guided statement about what you have seen, heard, or suspect, lovingly expressed to your child without expecting a response.
- *Unhealthy Concern*—concern expressed in anger or exaggeration with accusatory "you" statements, demanding a response and designed to manipulate circumstances or people to suit your own agenda.

"For this reason a man will leave his father and mother and be united to his wife, and they will become one flesh" (Gen.

2:24). When our children marry, we lose whatever control we had in their lives.

Although we may feel that our concern stems from wanting the best for our children and grandchildren, very often issues of control are at the root of our concern. The attitude seems to be: *We've learned a lot. We know how to do it now. If only we could run that family, everything would be better!* That, of course, is not godly grandparenting.

On the following pages are some situations that you might encounter. The situations in the first chart are presented with typical responses that demonstrate either unhealthy or healthy concern. On the second page following, additional situations are given to provide an opportunity for you to test your own responses.

The positives and negatives of how we respond to the circumstances of our children's and grandchildren's lives can make or break our relationship with them.

MEDDLING

Meddling is usually the result of unhealthy concern, and it causes such friction between family members that it can be very difficult to have a healthy relationship with the children. Far more serious than intervention in a disciplinary situation as discussed in the last chapter, meddling occurs when a grandparent crosses the line from caring to controlling.

Do not lose heart! God never allows a negative circumstance in our lives without allowing a way out of it.

As far as the east is from the west, so far has he removed our transgressions from us.

— Psalm 103:12

"Come now, let us reason together," says the Lord. "Though your sins are like scarlet, they shall be as white as snow"

— Isaiah 1:18

Healthy and Unhealthy Concern

Situation Seen, Heard, or Suspected	Unhealthy Concern	Healthy Concern	God's Concern
Your grandchild is not attending church.	You'd better get your spiritual life in order!	I'm concerned that you're not attending church. Do you feel like talking about it?	Deut. 31:11–13 Heb. 10:25
Your son-in-law is not looking for work.	Isn't it about time you got a job?	Is there something we can do to help you find just the right job?	1 Tim. 5:8 Exod. 23:12
Your daughter-in-law can't cook.	Didn't your mother teach you anything?	I've got some special recipes. Can you come over and try them out with me?	Prov. 31:10–28 Titus 2:3–5
Your grandchild lies.	I'm going to tell your parents!	We don't like lying here.	Prov.12:22; Lev. 19:11; Eph. 6:25
Your daughter does not discipline. (or reverse)	How can you let her get away with that? or You're too strict with the child!	Let's talk about when you were a little girl.	Prov. 23:13; 29:15; Col. 3:20; Eph. 6:1
The young family doesn't visit you.	I can't understand why you can't find some time to come over once in a while!	Have we done something wrong?	1 Pet. 3:8
The young family has money problems.	You got yourselves into this mess. Work it out.	We always have time to talk with you. I know there's a way to work it out.	Matt. 6:24

Healthy and Unhealthy Concern

Situation Seen, Heard or Suspected	My Response	God's Concern
Your daughter spanks and you don't. (or the reverse)		Eph. 6:4
Your grandchild is being neglected.		Ps. 127:3; Isa. 49:15
One of your grandchild's parents has been unfaithful.		Exod. 20:14; Col. 4:6 Eph. 4:29; Gal. 6:1
The young family has fast-food eating habits.		1 Cor. 6:19–20
Your grandchild is stressed from parental expectations.		Col. 3:21
The young family may move away.		Gen. 2:24; Prov. 3:5-6
Your grandchild is into cult worship.		Lev. 18:21; 19:26b, 31
Your grandchild watches too much TV.		1 Cor. 10:31
Your grandchild is allowed sweets anytime.		Dan. 1:8
(other)		

Meddling is not the unpardonable sin. There is a road back, a road to renewal and trust. If meddling occurs:

1. Stop blaming someone else. Own the problem.
2. Take responsibility verbally for what happened. Step firmly out of the role of "victim" into responsibility for past, present, and future actions.
3. Repent earnestly. Take authority and free yourself of meddling forever, saying that it will never happen again.
4. Ask forgiveness from God and those whom you wronged.

FORGIVENESS

When we *ask for forgiveness* of an adult child or grandchild for meddling in their lives, we accept God's instrument of grace— a way out, just as He promised. When we *extend forgiveness* to an adult child or grandchild who has disappointed or hurt us, we clear the debris from cracked relationships and make a way for the Holy Spirit to mend these relationships and minister in our lives.

We know deep down in our hearts if we have areas of unforgiveness that need to be addressed. During an unguarded moment we may find ourselves longing to hear the voice of an estranged loved one. We may ache for the touch of a distant child, a child who never comes. We yearn for restoration of happy times or, when that is not possible, at least closure to what has happened. By holding back forgiveness, we make the cracks in the relationship longer, wider, and harder for God to mend.

Do you need to ask forgiveness or extend forgiveness for something that has happened? If so, don't hold back. Ask God to show you the road back to wholeness and a right relationship with your children. Have you ever seen flowers growing from a stone? God, by His grace, can make it happen. He can make even the desert blossom like a rose. Someone has to start the process. Is that someone you?

Prayer

As Christians, there is one lesson we're supposed to have learned by now. It is that our first response to any situation should be prayer. When we forget that truth, we limit God and the blessings He wants to bestow upon us.

Prayer reminds us who is in control. Your life is not in that child or his or her parents. Your life is in Jesus Christ, and He is the one who validates your existence. It is not what you, your children, or your grandchildren do, but what Christ has done for you by His death on the cross that gives your life purpose. His all-sufficient grace and His restoration power are His free gifts to you. As long as we are looking to others for acceptance and love, we will be disappointed. We need to remind ourselves of what is true in terms of eternal life and act upon that.

Because most grandparents are in the latter stages of life, we need to focus on our prayer life. Prayer before taking action or responding is crucial. It is our first line of defense and our best offense. Pray when you get up, when you lie down, when you walk, or when you sit. Prayer is the bedrock of grandparenting. Wisely expressing concern for children and grandchildren *requires* prayer and must be measured against the Word.

GRACE PRINCIPLE:

God's grace awaits the repentant sinner.

Let the wicked forsake his way, and the unrighteous man his thoughts; let him return to the Lord, that he may have mercy on him, and to our God, for he will abundantly pardon.

— Isaiah 55:7, RSV

Grandparenting by grace requires that our concern for children and grandchildren be expressed in a loving way, even as our Father loves us.

Chapter 8

LOVE THAT HELPS, LOVE THAT HURTS

It is the desire of Christian grandparents to love their children and grandchildren in constructive, healthy ways. To help us achieve this goal, God provides frequent glimpses of the height and breadth and depth of His love for us to model and pass on to others. They are only glimpses, however, because His love is so vast, so all-encompassing, and so great, that we will never be able to completely comprehend it until we stand before Him.

GOD'S LOVE

God's divine love adorns our soul. Softly and tenderly, He wraps His love around us like we wrap our arms around a grandchild. Through the Scriptures, we see that God's love is His grace to us.

<u>By His love (grace), we are grandparents.</u>

May the Lord bless you from Zion all the days of your life;
may you see the prosperity of Jerusalem, and may you live to
see your children's children.

— Psalms 128:5–6

69

By His love (grace), we are sustained.

Even to your old age and gray hairs I am he, I am he who will sustain you. I have made you and I will carry you; I will sustain you and I will rescue you.

— Isaiah 46:4.

By His love (grace), we are saved.

But because of his great love for us, God, who is rich in mercy, made us alive with Christ even when we were dead in transgressions—it is by grace you have been saved.

— Ephesians 2:4–5

By His love (grace), we have eternal life.

My sheep hear my voice, and I know them, and they follow me; and I give them eternal life, and they shall never perish, and no one shall snatch them out of my hand. My Father, who has given them to me, is greater than all, and no one is able to snatch them out of the Father's hand.

— John 10:27–29, RSV

—

God's love has no beginning and no end. Even the grand-parent who has lived a life riddled with mistakes can know without a doubt there is still some of God's love in him or her, however damaged that life may be.

God's love does not depend upon our "goodness." Even the unforgivable sin of unbelief, when we repent and believe, does not destroy our ability to respond to God's love for us. God's love can never be completely lost.

T.W. Hunt teaches in his landmark L.I.F.E. course, *The Mind of Christ,* that the goal of God's love for us is oneness with Him. Hunt offers the following behavior comparisons, which are particularly relevant to a grandparent's love for a grandchild and the behavior of Christ.

Behavior of Love	*Behavior of Christ*
Suffers long	Luke 9:54
Is kind	Mark 6:48–50
Does not brag	John 5:30
Does not seek its own	John 6:15
Is not provoked	John 6:70
Rejoices in truth	Matthew 11:25
Bears all things	Luke 22:32
Believes all things	Luke 19:5
Hopes all things	Matthew 16:18
Endures all things	Matthew 26:53[1]

How can we respond to a love so great? By spreading His gift of love around in the family and putting His grace principles into practice in our daily associations. Think again about the hurtful effects of unhealthy concern outlined in the previous chapter and then about the many blessings we receive from healthy grandparenting concern. Just as with concern, love gets lost in issues of control.

Controlling Love	*Godlike Love*
Focuses on "me"	Focuses on "others"
Emphasizes "getting"	Gives to others
Demands	Discusses
Tears down	Builds up
Reacts	Responds
Is self-motivated	Is Christ-enabled
Retains bad feelings	Forgives
Ignores	Listens
Rejects criticism	Weighs criticism
Uses silence	Communicates

Ours is not the only way. Different isn't always wrong. Unlike God's free gift of unconditional, unfailing love, controlling love is self-centered. It aspires to power or popularity or self-gratification. Most relational problems in grandparenting are born out of confusion between control and power. The real power is in God-like love.

Let's examine two of the more serious problems that arise from confusion between control and power.

Spoiling Grandchildren

"John, if your mother gives the kids one more expensive present, you're going to have to have a talk with her!" Grandparents can confuse love with gifts. Some don't know when to quit. This compulsion might come from an inability to provide "things" for their own children as they were growing up. While this is understandable, lavishing gifts on grandchildren might cause resentment in the parent who was given little or nothing in childhood and now receives the same treatment as an adult.

Most parents don't mind a little spoiling, such as allowing a child an ice cream cone at the mall or buying a special gift just to say "I love you." Serious problems develop, however, when the spoiling is in direct opposition to a parent's wishes.

"Mom, I told you not to buy her that! I wanted her to keep saving for it!" Provoking such outbursts from parents undermines our credibility and trustworthiness. The result can be restricted contact and lost love.

It isn't just buying things that causes such rifts. Spoiling grandchildren by giving in to their wishes simply because a parent is not around, making secret pacts behind a parent's back, or asking a child "not to tell" send confusing signals to a child and can put a grandparent out in the cold.

Other important examples are when babysitting rules such as bedtimes and eating habits are not respected. We are a sure hit with the grandkids, but we're in the doghouse with their parents. Spoiling, when it gets out of hand, is just not worth the trouble it causes. There is no "grandparent right" to spoil a grandchild unless it is occasional and done in a lighthearted way in partnership with the parent.

"My daughter, Anne, lets me have a good time with my granddaughter," a friend said. "I spoil Angie until her mother tells me 'that's enough.' She knows how much Angie and I love and understand each other. You see, my granddaughter reminds me so much of Anne when she was little. I think of her as a gift to me from my daughter. I am just so grateful, I want to give back. Anne lets me do it, but I know my limits."

PLAYING FAVORITES

A friend of mine who adopted two boys tells this sad story:

> We got both of the children as infants and during the same year. Bradley is fair-haired and shy. Robby has lots of black hair and is roly-poly, always smiling and playful. When they are in the double stroller, passersby remark about the differences in the two brothers. They dote over Robby and pay little attention to Bradley. Even my parents do this. When they come over, they pay all of their attention to Robby and leave Bradley alone.
>
> This has continued now for two years. I see Bradley become more withdrawn with each visit from my parents. Can't they see what they are doing, favoring one sibling over another? Last week I finally told my mom that if she and Dad can't treat the boys equally and love them equally, they are not welcome in our home. They are really miffed, but I've told them often enough. I had to do it.

Favoritism is a dangerous game. It's understandable that one grandchild might steal your heart, but a grandparent must act carefully to protect the feelings and well-being of the sibling(s) or cousin(s). The other children need to be included.

One little boy put it this way when asked about his grandparents: "My sister always gets picked to do things with my grandparents. It's never me. They like her better than me." And don't you know that sister, who loves her brother, can tell something isn't right and feels guilty when she alone is chosen? Every child desires a grandparent's affection. They shouldn't be made to feel guilty for receiving it, nor should they experience the pain that comes when it is withheld or unequally given.

CONSEQUENCES OF LOVE THAT HURTS

The chart on the following page shows some of the devastating consequences when grandparent love is misguided or just plain wrong.

UNCONDITIONAL GRANDPARENT LOVE

In today's changing families, grandparents are faced with many kinds of frustrating, heart-touching challenges and surprises. Grandchildren come at any time and in varying conditions. The only constant is that every one of them needs all of the unconditional grandparent love they can get. Following the commandment from John 13:34, here are some suggestions for ways to show grandchildren unconditional love when it may not be easy.

The Distant, Unresponsive Grandchild.
- ❖ Draw the child out with strategic silence, listening, closeness, and patience.
- ❖ Build up the child with positive comments such as: "You are beautiful!" "I'm proud of you!" Expect no response. Be honest, because a child knows when we really mean what we say.

The Undisciplined Grandchild.
- ❖ Partner with the parents.
- ❖ Use some "tough love" principles in responding. "We don't allow that here! Would you rather just go home now,

Action	Reaction	Result	Alternative
Meddling	Anger • Distrust Hurt feelings • Confusion	Loss of respect Power struggles Disconnection	Cooperation
Spoiling	Delight • Happiness	High expectations Parent's wrath Inflated worth	Partnering with parents
Bragging	Embarrassment Disbelief	Less contact Lack of credibility	Honoring
Competing	Friction	Lost relationships Damaged marriages Turf battles	Partnering with grandparents
Criticizing	Shame • Frustration Embarrassment	Lost self-esteem Withdrawal Angry feelings	Accepting, Understanding, Affirming
Perfectionism	Frustration • Desperation Guilt • Feeling of failure	Distorted standards Suicidal thoughts	Modeling Christ
Improper Touching	Shame • Fear • Guilt	Lifetime shame Lifetime guilt Lifetime fear	Healthy touching

and we'll talk with your parents?" "I'll wait one minute for the *real* (child's name) to return. If he doesn't, this one will be sent to bed!"

❖ Do not take verbal, emotional, or physical abuse from a grandchild. Report it immediately to the parent(s) and love the child from a distance and by prayer until the behavior is gone.

The Grandchild with Destructive Habits.

❖ Do not excuse property damage. Report such behavior to the parent(s).

❖ If the habit is self-destructive (drugs, alcohol, tobacco), report it to the parents. Such matters are the parents' responsibility.

The Grandchild Who Dresses Funny.

❖ Understand and have patience with fads and trends. That is the same lovable child underneath the attention-getting facade, a child who wants to fit in with peers or perhaps is in a temporary rebellion. A child rebuffed by family often will go to even further extremes just to prove individuality. Chiding can backfire.

❖ Do not compliment the way they look. That lends credence to their sometimes outrageous attire.

❖ Do not take sides with the child against the parents' expressed concern over the attire.

The Grandchild with a Disability.

❖ Spend extra time with this child. Do the extra thing. Pour out your love. Look past the infirmity to the unique person within. Remind him or her of the Father's love.

❖ Take the disabled child on special outings when possible or bring the out-of-doors to him in the form of pine cones, ant farms, flowers, songs, poems, etc.

❖ Build self-esteem and confidence with your words and actions.

The Terminally Ill Grandchild

❖ Try never to allow the child to see the depth of your sorrow.

❖ Spend as much time as possible in prayer for this child.

❖ Support the parent(s) in their grief by being as strong as you can be in this ongoing time of crisis.

❖ Help with arrangements that may be too difficult for parents to accomplish. Be strong in the Lord.

❖ Bring into the child's life as much joy as you possibly can.

The Foster Grandchild

❖ Do not force attentions. Show patience in the relationship.

❖ Although the relationship may be temporary, a "grandparent" has a golden opportunity to instill values and shower love on a hurting child. Foster children who have grown to adulthood often tell about the impact such Christian caring made in their lives. Tell the child about the Lord and what He means to you, gently, lovingly. Not selling. Just telling.

The Adopted Grandchild

❖ Take your lead from the child until you are both comfortable. This is easier when the child is an infant, harder and more delicate when the child is adopted at an older age..

❖ Do not be afraid to show your grandparent love, especially if the child is preschool-aged or teenaged when the relationship begins. These children will be hungry for love.

❖ Always keep your place and follow the parents' plan. Be honest. The adopted child may be on guard, previously hurt, misguided, or neglected. Take your time.

The Mixed-Race Grandchild

❖ Every child is unique and loved by God. Acceptance, depending on the circumstances, may be difficult for a grandparent. Do your best to be unbiased, loving, and available. Do not judge.

The Grandchild Being Raised in Another Faith
❖ Live your Christian faith without compromise. Continue to prove the power of salvation with every word and deed.
❖ Do not criticize or ridicule the other faith. Say nothing. Silence speaks volumes.
❖ This is not grandparent business.
❖ Pray for your grandchild's salvation through Jesus Christ.

The Unexpected Grandchild
❖ Support the birth versus abortion.
❖ Support the parents in creating a strategy and plan for the birth of the baby and the future of the mother and father.
❖ Do not rush in with money or assistance unless requested.
❖ Love the new grandchild as Jesus does.

The Grandchild from a Previous Marriage
❖ Give the new relationship time. You don't have to pretend to love a "grandchild" from a previous marriage who is now part of your family. God will bless you with an honest feeling you can convey. Such a feeling will evoke a response from the child, usually warmth and even love.
❖ Understand mood changes. The child may have feelings of resentment, fear, or, at the very least, concern about how they will be received by extended family members.

Have you noticed something through these first seven chapters of *Grandparenting by Grace*? *A grandparent's main duty is to love.* We live out the role through changing relationships. We partner with parents regarding money or discipline. We teach godly values and model good habits. But the basis, the foundation for all that we do is *love*. By our love, God loves our grandchildren.

EVERLASTING LOVE

Loving grandchildren today can be complicated. We might cry out like Jeremiah, "O Lord . . . we are called by thy name; leave us not" (Jer. 14:9, RSV). Without the promise of everlasting love from our Heavenly Father, some of us would buckle under the emotion and stress. His sustaining, saving, tender love is everlasting. We know that from His Word:

- ❖ "'The eternal God is your refuge, and underneath are the *everlasting arms*'" (Deut. 33:27, italics added).
- ❖ "'Is not my house right with God? Has he not made with me an *everlasting covenant,* arranged and secured in every part? Will he not bring to fruition my salvation and grant me my every desire?'" (2 Sam. 23:5, italics added).
- ❖ "Surely he will never be shaken; *a righteous man will be remembered forever*" (Ps. 112:6, italics added).
- ❖ "For to us a child is born, to us a son is given, and the government will be on his shoulders. And he will be called Wonderful Counselor, Mighty God, *Everlasting Father,* Prince of Peace" (Isa. 9:6, italics added).
- ❖ "Do you not know? Have you not heard? The Lord is the *everlasting God,* the Creator of the ends of the earth. He will not grow tired or weary, and his understanding no one can fathom" (Isa. 40:28, italics added)
- ❖ "But Israel will be saved by the Lord with an *everlasting salvation;* you will never be put to shame or disgraced, to ages everlasting" (Isa. 45:17, italics added).
- ❖ "The ransomed of the Lord will return. They will enter Zion with singing; *everlasting joy* will crown their heads. Gladness and joy will overtake them, and sorrow and sighing will flee away" (Isa. 51:11).
- ❖ "'In a surge of anger I hid my face from you for a moment, but with *everlasting kindness* I will have compassion on you' says the Lord your Redeemer" (Isa. 54:8, italics added).
- ❖ "I have loved you with an *everlasting love* (Jer. 31:3, italics added).

O, Father, pour upon me Your boundless love.
Enter into my soul with Your grace
that I might be knit together with You by love.
Your grace is sufficient for me.
Draw me to Yourself, for I can do nothing by myself.
May my grandchildren see us as united.
May my grandchildren see Your matchless love through me.
In Jesus' name.

Amen.

GRACE PRINCIPLE:

We do not deserve God's grace.

But because of his great love for us, God, who is rich in mercy, made us alive with Christ even when we were dead in transgressions—it is by grace you have been saved.
— Ephesians 2:4–5

Next we learn some new ways to put our love to work—having fun with our grandchildren!

℘

PART THREE

Joy, Joy, Joy!

Grandma even lets me play dress up with her pretty clothes!"
"My grandpa tells the best stories about the olden days!" "I
have more fun at Grandma and Grandpa's house than any
other place in the whole world!"

What a wonderful season of life! Grandparents have all the
fun and none of the responsibility, or so we might think. And
in the brief span of their childhood, we seize blessed opportunities to share the joy of happy times with our precious grandchildren.

By His grace and through His Word, God has prescribed
joy for grandparents. Joy can come in the simplest of forms: a
silly game, a toothless smile, a happy song, an unexpected hug,
the smallest gesture of understanding and love. Or joy can
come in big packages: new birth, new skills, graduation, godly
marriage, and effective parenting.

Joy is God's gift of grace to grandparents for a job well
done.

℮

Chapter 9

HAVING FUN WITH GRANDCHILDREN

Grandpa Gene loves to baby-sit his grandson, Timmy, even though it tuckers him out trying to keep up with a three year old. One Sunday afternoon he and Timmy had played games on the living room floor, gone for a nice walk around the block, and eaten a peanut butter sandwich. Grandpa was weary and thought he'd just take a little catnap sitting up while Timmy was occupied with his toys. He leaned his head back against the sofa and closed his eyes. The plan was foiled almost immediately, however, when Timmy climbed up on his grandfather's lap. Smiling inside, Grandpa kept his eyes closed to see what Timmy would do. Timmy put both little hands on his grandfather's face. They felt warm and sweet. In the brief silence, he could feel Timmy breathing in and out against his cheek. Then, with great care, Timmy lifted up one of his Grandpa's eyelids and said softly, "Grandpa, are you in there? I'm out here and I don't have anybody to play with."

Who can resist such need? Yes, grandchildren *need* to play, and we are blessed when they want to play with us.

Oh, it can be tiring to have fun; we all know that. My mother used to say, "I love to see the children come, and I love to see them go." We knew she meant no disrespect. She had twenty-eight grandchildren, and sometimes she'd had enough fun!

You probably have hundreds of ideas for ways to have fun with grandchildren. Here are a few that I have accumulated from years of having fun with my own perfect grandchildren and from smart grandparents all over the country:

Stretch their imaginations

- ❖ Play "What if?" games that provoke thought and creativity.
- ❖ Ask questions that require complex answers.
- ❖ Write poems, plays, and stories.
- ❖ Read aloud. Put on a puppet show. Think up riddles.
- ❖ Role play, then reverse the roles. Play house.

Music

- ❖ Sing. Teach them how to play an instrument.
- ❖ Study musical composers and their techniques.
- ❖ Listen to music together. Write music and lyrics, and then make tapes of your compositions.

Arts and Crafts

- ❖ Sew. Do needlepoint. Crochet. Knit. Paint.
- ❖ Color. Practice wood-burning. Make papier-mâché. Sculpt.
- ❖ Make a scrapbook of paper and string.

Creative Bible Reading

- ❖ Read aloud together, one paragraph each.
- ❖ Role play: "I am Mary, and you are Martha." "You are David, and I am Goliath." Tell the story from a picture Bible.

Fun with Food

- ❖ Bake cookies. Decorate a cake. Go for fast food.
- ❖ Pop popcorn. Break lettuce for salad. Set the table.
- ❖ Bake bread. Learn about ethnic foods.
- ❖ Take gourmet cooking lessons. Celebrate at a restaurant.

Gardening

- ❖ Teach botanical facts. Get dirty together.
- ❖ Grow something from seed. Learn how to prune.
- ❖ Demonstrate garden watering and fertilizing techniques.
- ❖ Teach how to grow vegetables or fruits.
- ❖ Show how to cut flowers. Practice flower arranging.
- ❖ Learn how to care for houseplants.

Trips

- ❖ Take a grandchild on your vacation.
- ❖ Take a grandchild for a day trip or a weekend trip.
- ❖ Fly a long distance grandchild in for a week or for the summer. Travel to see a grandchild regularly.

Animal Fun

- ❖ Go to the zoo or the aquarium. Housebreak a pet together.
- ❖ Throw a stick or a frisbee for the dog to catch. Keep snakes.
- ❖ Show pets in contests. Teach horseback riding. Milk a cow.
- ❖ Raise bunnies. Clean a gerbil cage together. Raise rats.

Touches and Hugs

- ❖ Give butterfly kisses, Eskimo kisses, or big smacker kisses.
- ❖ Hold hands. Hold one finger. Rub stocking feet. Cuddle up.
- ❖ Rock in the rocking chair until one of you falls asleep.
- ❖ Give piggyback rides.

Holiday Fun

- ❖ Attend the church Christmas program or Easter celebration.
- ❖ Reinforce holiday traditions. Start new ones.
- ❖ Teach history on the Fourth of July. Take pictures every holiday, making a scrapbook that grows by the year.

Outdoor Fun

- ❖ Play baseball, tennis, horseshoes. Swim together.
- ❖ Listen to the sounds of nature. Attend sporting events.

- ❖ Go camping. Start a campfire with sticks. Pitch a tent.
- ❖ See the universe through a telescope.
- ❖ Walk through the woods naming foliage varieties.

Only-with-Grandpa Fun

- ❖ Make something from wood. Carve with a knife. Fly a kite.
- ❖ Tickle. Whistle. Drill. Saw.
- ❖ Play the harmonica. Make a bow and arrow.
- ❖ Make a slingshot. Climb a tree. Build a tree house.
- ❖ Have a man-to-man talk.

Just-for-the-Fun-of-It-Fun

- ❖ Jump in mud puddles. Make snow angels. Make a snow-man.
- ❖ Play pretend. Walk in the rain. Talk about the joy of being a child of God.

Make a Train Cake

Many of my twelve perfect grandchildren have had a train cake made by Grandma. They are easy and are a smash hit at a grandchild's birthday celebration. Moms love them. Here's how to make one.

Save six or eight cardboard juice cans. Buy a cake mix that is the child's favorite. Locate a large cookie sheet or piece of wood about 20" x 20" on which to place the train. Cover the sheet with foil. On the foil, lay a "track" of black licorice the way you want the train to go.

Grease and flour the inside of the juice cans. Mix the cake as directed and spoon cake mix into each can to half full. Bake the filled juice cans at 350° for about twenty minutes or until the mix shows dry at the top of the can.

Let each can of cake cool, and then shake it out carefully. Cover each with vanilla frosting and lay each "train car" on the licorice "track." Connect each one to the other with a short piece of black licorice.

Now comes the fun of decorating each train car. The engine requires a black licorice chimney. The other cars need gumdrop windows. All the cars need round peppermint wheels, four to a car, hugging the frosting and perched on the black licorice "track." The caboose is especially important. It should be of red frosting, bringing up the rear with any special decoration your heart desires. Almost always, the birthday grandchild wants the caboose!

You can write the child's name on the engine or buy a candle that illustrates the age of the child and put it right in the middle of the train.

Place a few drops of diluted green food coloring in one cup of fresh shredded coconut. Mix well, and it becomes grass to go around the track. Place figures on the grass: animals, cowboys, a farm scene, a zoo, whatever your grandchild would like to see from the window of a passing make-believe train.

When the time comes to serve the birthday cake, the children at the party will ask for their own personal favorite: the baggage car, the passenger car, the engine, the cattle car, or whatever. They will love having their own piece of the train and track with a side car of ice cream.

Very often, moms, especially working moms, are too busy to make birthday cakes special for youngsters. This is something we can do that takes the load off Mom and says to a grandchild, "Grandma loves you! Happy Birthday!"

A Special Outing

Fun with grandchildren might mean taking them on a special outing. Here is an idea that combines learning with the fun of anticipation of the trip.

When each of my perfect grandchildren reaches age three, it's time to go shopping with Grandma. Then we go once a year thereafter.

First, Grandma makes a date with the grandchild and gives advance notice to the parents. The child wears his or her

Sunday best, because our time together begins with lunch—not a fast food lunch but at a favorite sit-down restaurant. At lunch, the child and Grandma look the menu over, and the child places his or her order. Napkins are placed on laps. When lunch arrives, thank you's are said to the server and to God. The child eats with a fork and knife and asks for salt or pepper, "please." After lunch, Grandma and child figure the tip, and Grandma gives the child money to pay the bill, after which thank you's are repeated.

Then, it's off to the mall for two "needs" and one "want."

The child's two needs are decided ahead with the parents. They range from new jeans to a pair of tennis shoes to a white dress shirt and tie. The one "want" is the child's heart's desire, within reason: one thing he or she wants very much. It might be a bag of candy, a new pair of party shoes, or the latest sports poster. (No expensive video games.)

Ideally, the limit on the two needs is twenty dollars each and ten dollars on the one want. Don't let your grandchild coerce you into more purchases or more expensive purchases. I *never* do. Well, almost never.

This outing teaches manners that the child may or may not learn at home. It teaches the value of money; we discuss the cost of lunch as well as the price of the two "needs" and one "want." It teaches the difference between "wanting" and "needing," a valuable lesson a child will carry into adulthood.

The children look forward to going out with Grandma. They really get excited. Parents love it. I try to plan it just before the start of the school year to help out with the high cost of outfitting the children while we have a wonderful time to-gether.

Everybody benefits, especially Grandma. I have years of blessed memories of these special outings. Once I was able to take two of our granddaughters with me. Amy and Michelle are almost the same age. They are very close friends. (Now, these are two adorable girls! I don't tell you that because they are my grandchildren, you understand.)

They were both about nine years old. On our trip to the mall, we went to the shoe store where both girls wanted the same black patent party shoes. People in the shoe department noticed how the girls enjoyed each other's company.

The clerk had the shoes in Michelle's size, but sadly announced she didn't have the same style in a half size larger for Amy. Michelle pleaded with the clerk to go look one more time. The good-natured clerk said she would. Hearing that, Michelle jumped up and disappeared around the corner. I quickly followed to find her bent down by a large plant, hands together under her chin, praying aloud, "Lord, please let her find Amy's size. Pleeese, Lord?" Then Michelle ran back to sit beside Amy. Out came the clerk with the shoes in Amy's size in her hand! The jubilant girls exchanged high fives and danced around as Michelle yelled, "Thank You, Lord!" Everyone around us laughed, enjoying their joy. It was a very special outing.

I've been taking my grandchildren on this special yearly outing for many years. I figure that pretty soon the older ones will start taking me. Maybe.

Make Something Together

There is a special pleasure in making something for someone and special pleasure in receiving a handmade gift. Grandchildren enjoy making things with their hands, particularly under the direction of a loving grandparent.

Make a Picture Frame

Our granddaughter, Olivia, gave us an odd-sized picture of herself, encased in a homemade frame only she could have created. It is red, green, yellow, blue, and her favorite color, purple. It is a frame that could never be found in a store. It's one-of-a-kind!

When a grandchild is at your house, you can make a picture frame together for Mom, for Dad, for brother or sister, or for a little friend. All it takes is a few crayons, some heavy paper or light wood, and a little imagination.

Make a Light Switch Cover

Ask the parent to give you the light switch cover from your grandchild's room or playroom. Together, you and your grandchild can cover it with a scrap of unused wallpaper. Glue and glitter help. Decorate it with paint or crayon if you desire. You might be able to collaborate with mom to match the wallpaper in the grandchild's room. Add excitement to the project by suggesting it as a surprise gift to mom. She'll love it!

Make a Pencil or Pen Holder

You can turn a small can into a useful tool. Cut colored paper to fit, and glue it around the can. Decorate it with crayon or paint, and cover the bottom with felt. These make great gifts for a grandchild to give a friend or sibling at birthday time. And they make it themselves—with a little help from you!

Make a Calendar

Fill in the squares of a plain calendar with event days, birthdays, and anniversaries specific to your grandchild's family. Have your grandchild add his or her own unique artistic effects to the days you mark. This is a beautiful and helpful gift from the child to parents.

Make a Book

Children love to make books. They can make scrapbooks of pictures they have collected. They can write and illustrate stories. They can make a small photo album of a trip or of their pet. All you need are sheets of paper, heavier sheets for the covers, and yarn or staples to hold the book together. Make a recipe book of your grandchild's favorite dishes. Use your own handwriting and your grandchild's handwriting, however primitive. Trust me. It will be a treasure for any mom.

Teach Gift Wrapping

This kind of fun takes patience. Once mastered, it is a skill with great value at holiday time. Start by teaching them how to fold paper around the corners of a box. The next challenge is teaching how to tie the package for an attractive look. Buy spools of colored ribbon, and teach the child how to make bows. Fabric stores offer easy instructions.

You can make paper chains, bean bags, hand-printed sweatshirts, stencils, or puppets. It doesn't matter what it is. What matters is that you and your grandchild made a special gift for someone you both care about. And you did it together!

ENJOY THE OUTDOORS

Summer is a wonderful time to be outside with grandchildren. Long, happy moments can be spent just blowing the furry tops off mature dandelions. Tell the child that a blessing is a special wish. Encourage the child to send a blessing to someone special and then blow the blessing to them on the wings of the dandelion.

Judy Gattis Smith's book, *Grandmother Time,* is filled with good ideas for fun outdoors. Judy reminds us that pussy willows, for instance, are good for feeling, very softly. Look at a flower and see it looking back at you! Flowers with faces like pansies or Johnny-jump-ups offer endless possibilities. See how many kinds of trees or different colored wildflowers you can find. You might get a book on wildflowers in your area, and use it as your guide on a treasure hunt.

If you run out of outdoor ideas, find a tree to lie under. Find the many shades of green you can identify. Look up through the tree to the sky through unhurried, careful eyes. You and your grandchild have enough to hurry about. Here's a good chance to be a listener in your grandchild's noisy world. And the memories you share will last a lifetime.[1]

WHEN HAVING FUN IS HARD WORK

You may be thinking, *I'd like to have fun like that with my grandchildren, but they're not here! I'd like to play with them, but they don't want to play with me. I'd like to feel joy and happiness when I am with them, but it isn't always possible.*

Keeping in mind that God wants us to experience the joy of grandparenting, let's look at some things we can do when these circumstances arise.

Long-Distance Fun

In this highly mobile society, more and more grandparents find themselves grandparenting children who live far away. We can't relieve the ache in our hearts from missing them, but there are things we can do to have fun and keep our relationship thriving and growing. Here are a few ideas just for fun.

1. Send pictures of yourself and/or your spouse in a particularly funny situation. (For example: The garden hose broke. Grandpa got all wet and looked like this.)
2. Cut out newspaper comic strips. White out the words and write in your own. Mail them to your grandchild.
3. Pre-address envelopes. Write and mail notes on sacks, napkins, or whatever is available wherever you are and whenever you think of your grandchild.
4. Send the program from a sporting event you attended with your comments about the game.
5. Send riddles. Ask your grandchild to guess the answers. Include a small stamped, self-addressed envelope.

They Don't Want to Play with Me

Another reason God has allowed us to grow older is to give us time for His wisdom to sink in. What's going on when a child says, "I don't want to play"? Something is happening in the child's life that says, "You shouldn't have fun. You're a bad child. You did a bad thing today. What's the use of having fun, anyway? Why do I have to play with my grandparents?"

There can be many reasons for such a response to your honest, loving approach. Be patient. We do not know what might have happened to that child today, yesterday, or for many yesterdays that causes them to reject even you.

Fun when Finances Are Low

It's hard to think of having fun when you can't afford it. But everything we do with our grandchildren does not have to cost money. Here are some things you can do with grandchildren that are free or don't cost much.

Going for a walk	Making a meal together
Homemade crafts	Daydreaming
Sharing hobbies	Cleaning the garage together

Fun with Physical Limitations

We've all said it at one time or another: "I'm not as young as I used to be!" However, we can still have fun with grandkids, even though we may not be as mobile as we once were. Here are some quiet activities.

Reading together	Telling stories
Recalling family history	Playing board games

Different Parenting Styles

Ever feel like you were walking on eggshells around a daughter or daughter-in-law because of style differences in how children are raised? It's hard to have fun when you don't agree with the parents' rules. But it is a control issue, and the parents are in charge of the children. We have to be creative when parents have set boundaries on what we are allowed to do and where we are allowed to go with *their* kids.

Understanding that different isn't always wrong, we part-ner with the parents. When we do that we find that trust increases over time, and boundaries ease up a little. At best, we are able to bring joy to the children and take some home with us by God's grace.

I'm Too Busy to Have Fun!

Both grandparents and grandchildren say that today. Grandparents who do not yet have the luxury of living com-fortably on retirement income or are working a part-time or full-time job may find scheduling time for fun with grandchil-dren difficult. Conversely, grandchildren are occupied with school, friends, home responsibilities, or outside jobs and forget that spending happy time with Grandma and Grandpa is important and good for them.

A grandparent is never too busy for a quick phone call or to leave a short note behind after a visit. I know a grandmother who puts a note under her grandson's pillow just before she leaves his home. The child finds it at bedtime. The note usually says something like, "Your Fairy Grandmother was here. Sleep well. I love you every day. I'll call you Tuesday."

Fun That Fits Their Ages and Interests

Fun with grandchildren can be limited if we aren't aware of what interests or excites a child as he or she grows. For example, behavior at an upscale restaurant could be noisy and even embarrassing if you take a two-year-old. And a teenager might be pretty bored by a walk in the woods or a game of checkers. A little thoughtful planning ensures that the child can act his or her age. And they will! Plan your fun like you plan a doctor's appointment. Mark the calendar. It's that important.

Fun with Infants:

- ❖ Cuddling. Singing. Feeding. Rocking.

Fun with Preschoolers

❖ Physical games. Walks. Reading. Playing house.

Fun with Elementary Age Children

❖ Movies. Videos. Plays. Sports. Activities. Crafts. Food.

Fun with Teenagers

❖ Videos. Trips. Music. Food. Food. Food. Food.

Having fun with grandchildren at any age makes wonderful memories. Playing enhances their sense of fun and yours! It unleashes creativity, teaches motor skills, encourages quick thinking, and can wear you out. Whether it is a quiet board game, a trip down the pool slide, or hitting a home run, grandparents who take the time to understand and appreciate their grandchildren for who they are at their age and interest level will have more successful happy times to remember.

Playing and having fun with grandkids can make a lasting imprint on their lives. Eighteen-year-old Arlene keeps a picture of her Grandpa playing baseball with her on the mirror in her dorm room at college. Many young parents will pass on to their children the games played with their own grandparents. What a great God is He who rewards us with treasured memories just for having fun! Such memories are expressions of God's grace.

INCLUDING OTHERS IN THE FUN

Whenever possible, ask your grandchildren's parents to join in the fun: playing a game, going to a sporting event, enjoying a stage play, even just taking a walk. Ask them to come along. When you do, you're saying, "We're a family! I love you!" And it adds to the fun!

Remember that little sister or big brother doesn't like being left out. If a fun time is meant just for one child, ask the parents to explain to the sibling(s) so there will be no hurt feelings.

HONORING GOD WHILE YOU'RE HAVING FUN

Honesty. Integrity. Fairness. These are as much a part of fun with grandchildren as being with them. Here's a chance to show your grandchildren what the Christian faith stands for and to demonstrate other principles they can take with them for the rest of their lives. Ask yourself, *how would Jesus play with my grandchildren ?*

GRACE PRINCIPLE:

God's grace is a source of joy.

Satisfy us in the morning with your unfailing love, that we may sing for joy and be glad all our days.
— Psalm 90:14

Having fun with grandchildren is fleeting joy. They grow up quickly. Are you recording the blessings?

❦

Chapter 10

JOURNALING WHAT THEY SAY AND DO

O h, that's a good one! I must write that down."

"I can't remember. I should have written it down!"

Grandchildren can say and do the funniest, heart-touching things, sometimes when you least expect them. Journaling transforms these easily forgotten gems into tangible memories you and others can enjoy for many years to come.

Journaling simply means writing it down, keeping a record. It doesn't have to be fancy or require a great deal of planning. Some grandparents have boxes of corners of paper, old napkins, and cards on which they have written some wonderful things a grandchild did or said. They scribble on anything that is handy before the thought gets away.

OUT OF THE MOUTHS OF GRANDCHILDREN

No matter how you accomplish the task of recording what grandchildren say and do, if you do get in the habit, and if you do it long enough, it might just end up in print. *Out of the Mouths of Grandchildren* is a small volume of sayings and prayers spoken by my twelve perfect grandchildren and others I collected over the years. To give you an idea of how much fun this can be for you and your family, here are a few from that 1993 book plus some new ones.[1]

Wrong Party!

Anytime you have a number of perfect grandchildren in the same room at the same time, a squabble or two is inevitable. Nine-year-old Jeremy was at the bottom of the heap when Grandpa went over to break up the argument. As Grandpa began to settle them down, Jeremy popped up with hands on hips to say, "What do you mean, settle this in a democratic way? I'm a Republican!"

Nice Try

Grandpa Ross enjoys teaching his grandson the value of money and the importance of saving. He realized he had made a strong impression on seven-year-old Michael, when Michael came up with this great idea: "I know, Grandpa! I save one dollar, and then you match it. Then you give me two extra for being such a good boy. Now, that's a good deal, isn't it?"

I Love You, Too!

Grandpa Leo had his five-year-old grandson, Aaron, for a whole Saturday. It had been a busy day. Aaron and his grandfather have a special bond of love, and Leo had packed the day with experiences he thought Aaron might enjoy. As darkness fell, he reluctantly returned Aaron to his parents. After the customary big warm hug and promises to see each other soon again, Aaron chirped, "I must have been a good boy today, Grandpa. I only saw your eyebrows go straight once!"

Surprise, Surprise!

Grandma Ellen had planned carefully for her friend Martha's seventieth birthday party. She was glad her five-year-old granddaughter, Cassie, would be staying with her and she could show her off at the party. Grandma and Cassie made a big cake with a "70" on it. Cassie put on her Sunday dress, and

Martha arrived. Thinking her beautiful little granddaughter would be just the person to greet the guest of honor, Grandma sent Cassie to the door. The door opened and Grandma Ellen heard her granddaughter ask, "Are you seventy?" "Why, yes I am, dear," said the gracious guest of honor. To which Cassie responded, "Wow! Did you start with one?"

Growing Up

Thirteen-year-old Annie had been away and hadn't seen her grandparents for over a year. When she arrived at their house, she dashed into the once-familiar kitchen, pulled up short, put her hands to her mouth, and exclaim, "Look, Grandma! Your counters got shorter!"

Thanks a Lot!

Bobby crawled up on his grandfather's lap and nestled his head into Grandpa's chest. Grandpa loved to hold him close. He put his arms around the little boy and laid his head against Bobby's soft, sweet-smelling hair. He was enjoying Grandparent Heaven, eyes closed, rocking back and forth with his precious grandson, when Bobby purred, "Tell me a story about the olden days when you played with the dinosaurs."

Close Enough

Six-year-old Jerod had tried so hard to memorize his part in the prayer of Jesus from the Sermon on the Mount for the Sunday School program. Each child had two lines to speak. His were especially important, because they were the first. (Our Father Who art in heaven, hallowed be Thy Name.) Up he stepped to the microphone and out came, "Our Father Who art in heaven, how do you know my name?"

Second Verse

David worked for days on the same prayer as Jerod. His two lines came near the very end. (And forgive us our trespasses as we forgive those who trespass against us.) Waiting in line, nervously twisting his sleeve, David stepped to the mike. Out of his mouth came, "And forgive us our trash baskets as we forgive those who put trash in ours."

A Grandchild's View

Teaching creative writing to an elementary school class, I closed with a question about grandparenting. I asked, "How do you know your grandmother loves you?" A little boy in the back of the room waved his hand with enthusiasm. When I called on him, he said, "I know my Grandma loves me 'cause when I look in her eyes, I can see all the way to her heart."

First Rights

It was time to be tucked in at Grandma and Grandpa's house. Six-year-old Michelle liked to say her prayers privately. Grandma leaned into the doorway and heard her granddaughter bless everyone she could think of, including the cat. Then Michelle closed by saying, "And dear God, if You decide You need my Grandma in heaven, please ask me about it first."

Help!

In Sunday School, Peter was learning about the Philistine giant killed by David in 1 Samuel. Following the lesson, the teacher asked questions to see if the children had understood the message of the story. She asked young Peter how he would have felt if he were faced with the giant. Peter responded, "If I was David and I had to fight Goliath, I'd call 911!"

I could go on and on as I'm sure you could, if you are a grandparent. In these examples of what comes out of the mouths of grandchildren, I have elaborated the details of the stories. You can do that, too. But, if there is no time and you want to record what was said quickly, just grab any piece of paper and jot down the essence of the story, such as "I'd call 911," or "I'm a Republican!" That will help you remember and you can fill in the joyful details later.

WHAT TO DO WITH YOUR JOURNAL

Don't let your pieces of paper hide in a closet or drawer only to be found after you're gone. Make a project of it.

- ❖ Ask a grandchild or an adult child to help you type them up into a Keepsake Notebook. This would be a unique gift to the child's parents or to the grandchild when he or she becomes a parent.
- ❖ Write them in a photo album alongside pictures of the grandchild at the time the words were spoken or the deed was done.
- ❖ Send some of your gems to the local newspaper.
- ❖ Give some to your church office for printing in the Senior's Newsletter.
- ❖ Stationery stores offer plain or fancy books filled with blank pages. Such a book, placed in a strategic spot in your house or carried in your purse or pocket, would be a handy way to journal what your grandchild says and does.
- ❖ Allow a professional to read them to see if they should be printed in book form.

Journaling what they say and do is lots of fun. Done with love and consistency, such a record can be a happy blessing for many generations to come. Why not start today?

GRACE PRINCIPLE:

By God's grace, joy is preserved.

Oh, that my words were recorded that they were written on a scroll.
— Job 19:23

The joy of grandparenting is enhanced when kids and grandkids live nearby, as we learn in the next chapter.

❦

Chapter 11

GRANDPARENTING CLOSE UP

Grandparents who can pick up the phone and talk to a son or daughter without dialing an area code, or drop by to pick up a grandchild for a day or a weekend of fun times together, are truly blessed. Growing up in a large family, I know how much it means to draw on that love, that support, that joy.

My dear mother learned her lessons well from Grandma Burch. She exhibited the patience of Job with up to eleven of us in the house. Dad worked on two-year contracts in foreign countries as a construction comptroller for an international development firm. Each of us was born two years apart. You guessed it! He missed most of our births and most of our graduations.

Two of my siblings died in infancy from diseases easily treated today. Mom raised the surviving nine of us through World War II and other crises such as measles, chicken pox, and mumps. I remember being quarantined in one room for weeks with sisters and brothers with chicken pox.

Then along came the twenty-eight grandchildren, most of them during the years in America's history that redefined the job of grandparenting—the sixties and seventies. Grown grandchildren showed up on my mother's doorstep, sometimes late at night. She sheltered and fed them. Children of divorce took up residence with her. She cooked and cleaned, providing a temporary, safe, loving environment for the children of broken families. A child calling in need of money always got it, although my mother had little to spare.

Problems can be found in most large families, and ours was no exception. But we all got together to celebrate holiday times at the three-story house on Harrison Street where most of us were raised. There were always about a dozen squirming, hungry, happy, unhappy, irresistible little kids underfoot. My brothers and sisters and I marveled at how Mom took it all in stride. She found the time and the patience to feed us royally, have fun with the children, and allow them to have fun with each other. A more gracious grandmother never lived!

It was really my mom who taught me that there are two kinds of grandparenting time.

Standard Time and Mountain Time

Standard Time is doing what we have to do to get by as a grandparent: enjoying the grandchildren when we see them; doing our duty because we have the job. If you are on Standard Time with your grandchildren, you are missing some of the greatest blessings of your life. Strive for the mountaintop.

Mountain Time is the highest quality of grandparenting time—teaching the children from our own life experiences, sharing knowledge from a career of thirty or forty years, asking questions to stimulate their minds and make learning fun.

Grandpa Endicott has devoted his grandparenting season to teaching the grandchildren something at every opportunity. When our grandson, Jeremy James, was small, he learned about God's universe from his grandpa. My husband had three careers. One of them was as a television producer/director of space documentaries. He taught Jeremy about the planets, beginning with the one closest to the sun. Using his knowledge of animals, when my husband and a grandchild visit the zoo, he takes time to teach the difference between the carnivores and herbivores. Grandpa Endicott's gifts to the grandchildren at birthdays or Christmas are usually learning tools such as books, charts, or other educational helps.

Hard as we try, though, it may not work out right everytime. One day Grandpa Endicott was woodworking in his shop with our grandson, Adam, who was then about eight years old. Thinking he would start a casual conversation about the future, my husband asked the standard question, "Adam, what are you going to be when you grow up?" Adam pondered the question for a bit, then stopped hammering, looked up at his grandfather, and said, "What do you care, Grandpa? You're gonna be dead then anyway!"

TOGETHERNESS

Has this ever happened to you? "Oh, hi, Mom. Glad you're home. Hope you can watch the kids. Give Billy a bath, and Betsy needs her hair washed, and take a look at Sammy's hand. I don't think he'll need stitches. We'll try to be back by 12:30 or 1:00. Have fun!"

Have fun??

If you have a daughter or son who relies on you as a free babysitter, you know that grandparenting close up can occasionally be a mixed blessing.

Here are some of the situations that can arise when living close to grandchildren.

Babysitting

"Suffer the little children to come unto me" (Matt. 19:14) is a theme for grandparents. We want to see those babies, but do we have to suffer to do it? Baby-sitting is an area of close-up grandparenting that cries for boundaries! Theirs and yours.

Lack of advance notice to Grandma can take all the joy out of babysitting. If it happens to you, have a loving talk with your grandchild's mother. Allowing it to happen time and time again only makes it more difficult to stop. Let them know, gently, and lovingly, that you have a life of your own.

Sometimes the mothers of our grandchildren assume that we know more than we do. Grandparents can make innocent mistakes because they haven't been told about the latest rule at the child's house. Caring parents will usually outline their rules for babysitters. But as my Grandpa used to say, "You'd better know what they is!"

Grandparents might have some physical limitations. No matter how good our health may be, sixty isn't twenty and seventy is nowhere near forty. Weak backs, bad knees, and stiff joints can spell trouble for eager babysitters.

Discipline can be a problem for grandparents when our kids have not taught their kids how to behave. Hard-to- handle grandchildren refuse to mind, reject correction, destroy your home, bother the neighbors, and embarrass you in public.

If you are going to supply this free service, follow these easy steps.

- ❖ Request a twenty-four-hour notice when your services are needed.
- ❖ Make sure you understand your daughter's or daughter-in- law's instruction, especially if her parenting methods differ from yours. If you are not sure about such things as foods, bedtimes, and television viewing, ask for a list so you can reinforce her desires with the children.
- ❖ Let your kids know what you can and can't do physically. Be honest about it. Don't hold back, trying to be nice.
- ❖ If lack of discipline shows up too often, it's time to have a talk with the parents about the fact that the grandkids need some instruction before they come over again.

Suffer the little children to come unto Grandma and Grandpa . . . with advance notice, with the cooperation of parents who provide a list of food and bedtime routines, with an honest understanding of what you can do for them, and with a promise that problem behavior has been resolved.

Helping Out in a Crisis

This is a time when all the rules go out the window, and everybody pitches in. Grandparents are thankful to be close enough to help in times of crisis. Godly grandparents let it be known that they can be called upon at any time.

Emmalyn lives in southern California. Her only daughter and two grandchildren live in Northridge, near Los Angeles. When the devastating earthquake hit in 1994, Emmalyn spent ten hours trying, in vain, to reach her daughter by telephone. She then got into her car and drove to her daughter. Arriving near the affected area, she, too, experienced chilling aftershocks from the quake. She was not allowed into the area where her daughter lived but made frantic inquiries and found the family in a shelter nearby. Emmalyn, her daughter, and two frightened children made the trip back to Grandma's house, where they rested and had a chance to regroup and plan.

Unlike a babysitting assignment, a crisis demands flexibility. Smaller crises might be an unexpected trip to the airport, an accident, a health emergency, or bad weather.

Helping out in a crisis is grandparenting by grace under fire. It is always the right thing to do.

Mentoring Young Parents

Living near young parents is a rewarding experience for grandparents who are willing to mentor. Mentoring means to tutor, coach, counsel, or guide. For Christian grandparents, mentoring is what Christ did and what God's Word does for us. More than helping out, mentoring has staying power. A mentor is committed to the task at hand.

If you are blessed to be near a family just starting out, I encourage you to become a mentor. Let your daughter or daughter-in-law know of your desire to teach her from your

years of experience in cooking, housekeeping, furniture arranging, scheduling, and child-rearing. Move into the relationship slowly, always mindful of the young parent's dignity. Tell
her you love her and would be honored to be her partner as
she learns the intricacies of being a homemaker, wife, and
mother. Grandpa can also be a mentor, making himself available to his son or son-in-law for car repair, plumbing problems, roof leaks, etc.

Many young couples need mentoring. As grandparents,
our focus is on our grandchildren. We want to see them grow
up in a healthy, responsible, God-fearing home with contented
parents. Mentoring their parents in a nonthreatening, loving
manner benefits your grandchild(ren) and creates a bond
between the two families that will never be broken.

Supporting the Single Working Mom

Grandmothers with time to spare can provide a service for
the single working mother that no one else can provide. Besides parents, no one loves, cares about, protects, and nurtures
a child like a grandparent. It's a one-of-a-kind love that makes
us the best possible day-care provider.

Single working mothers need all the help they can get. If
day care is not required of you:

- ❖ Pray for her every morning.
- ❖ Provide a homemade casserole once a week.
- ❖ Offer to clean house or run errands.
- ❖ Pick up the children for an afternoon or day of fun.
- ❖ Pick up the family for church.
- ❖ make yourself available to listen to plans, hopes, and
  dreams, and counsel when asked.
- ❖ Understand the stresses of the working mom's life. Antici-
  pate them and be a source of stability.

Margery and her mom have a weekly date for a back rub.
"My mom gives the best back rubs in the world! It sounds like

a little thing, but a back rub from Mom refreshes me. I begin again. It's more than a physical thing. Somehow, it soothes my head and my heart in the process. I absolutely love her for it!"

Honoring Boundaries

Just one more word here about partnering with parents. Remember that too much grandparenting is not normal. Living close by does not give a grandparent the right to become overinvolved. Possessiveness, too many announced and unannounced visits, and overbuying all can overwhelm and anger a young family and close the gate to grandchildren. Keeping communication flowing freely, taking helpful criticism well, and other helps are worth reviewing in chapters 6 and 7.

THE UNINVOLVED GRANDPARENT

"I don't know my grandparents. Other kids talk about theirs. I have some, but I don't know them. I wish I did." Debbie is seventeen. She lives ninety miles from her grandparents and has never seen them. She has been robbed of one of the most cherished bondings in a family. "I wish I did" is a word picture of her pain.

We have learned that the grandparent is central to the family. We are ancestors, historians, mentors, and emotional foundations. When that bond is broken, everyone suffers.

The Adult Child Suffers

One mother told me that she approaches obvious mother/daughter shoppers at the supermarket in her town and tells them how blessed they are to be able to shop together.

"At first they think I'm a little goofy, but then I tell them my mom never misses the Cannes Film Festival or Wimbledon, but she has missed all six of my daughter's birthdays. I usually shed a tear. They thank me, saying they will be more aware of the blessing of being together."

The Grandchild Suffers

"My grandma is great. She's a lot of fun. But she's too busy to see me very much. I miss her a lot." Jeffrey expresses what many children feel when grandparents are inconsistent or unavailable. Contemporary grandparents leading a busy life are challenged to find the right balance in family relationships.

The Grandparent Suffers

"I don't care for my daughter-in-law." "I'm not ready to be a grandparent." "I'm just too busy to get over there."

The grandparent who allows her own feelings about a parent, herself, or her schedule to cause her not to see a grandchild is out of focus. It is the child who loses. And Grandma is missing out on some of the greatest times she will ever have. Such all-around distress is unnecessary and hurtful. When honest conversation takes place and short-sightedness is replaced with a long-term, orderly plan, everybody wins. Sharing your interesting, wonderful self with grandkids is grandparenting by grace. There are thousands of long-distance grandparents who would gladly trade places with uninvolved grandparents who live close to their grandchildren.

GRACE PRINCIPLE:

God's grace is a gift.

For it is by grace you have been saved, through faith—
and this not from yourselves, it is the gift of God.
— Ephesians 2:8

Close up or far away, grandparenting by grace means ministering to the needs of those we love, our sisters and brothers in Christ and the community at large which may be needing the gifts of grace God has given specifically to you.

ॐ

Chapter 12

GRANDPARENTING AS A MINISTRY

My grandmother, Alice Mae McClelland Burch, daughter of a Presbyterian minister, married John Shepherd Burch, September 15, 1880, at age thirteen. She gave birth to their seventeen children in the log house built by her husband in Deer Lodge, Montana. Hers was not an easy life.

I can still see the old wood stove and the wood floor of the little log house where all those children were born and raised. I remember how she labored over the washboard out on the back porch until her knuckles were red and the veins on the back of her hands stood out from the strain of hand-wringing and hanging up clothes for as many as seventeen kids. She used crude implements to accomplish other tasks, both routine and difficult.

Skilled at nursing, she not only added my mother and her sixteen siblings to the Deer Lodge population, but she brought most of the townspeople into the world as well. Grandma taught her nine daughters how to sew, cook, and make roses, carnations, and mums out of painted paper and wire—flowers that looked like the real thing! The girls sold them on the street corners of downtown Deer Lodge to help support the large family and to buy a Christmas present for their parents.

Grandma would sit in the rocking chair that Grandpa made for her and tell fascinating stories about Indians, about surviving the elements, and about the many times God's grace manifested itself in the trying times in her life. What I remember best about my grandmother is that she loved Jesus. She came as close to the Proverbs 31 woman of the Bible as anyone I have ever known, as testified to in this excerpt from the *Montana Star Bulletin* newspaper story of April 24, 1948, on the occasion of her eightieth birthday celebration:

> Mrs. Burch has 121 living direct descendants including her 17 children, 59 grandchildren, 42 great-grandchildren and two great-great-grandchildren. She has spent her life devoting her time and thought to her home and family. Although she has never taken part in fraternal or social affairs, her life has been a full one and her reward is rich indeed in the love of her family and affection and admiration of her many friends. Never too busy to go to a neighbor in illness or distress, opening her home and sharing her table with all those who entered her door, Mrs. Burch represents the best of womankind and her gracious and kindly nature has reached beyond her doors into the lives of many in her community.[1]

My beloved grandmother lived her life in service to her family, her community, and her God. God poured His grace abundantly upon her, and it radiated out over nearly a century. It affects even you today by this writing. Through my grandmother's life, God is saying to us, "You also were saved to serve one another, to love one another, even as Jesus Christ loves you."

The expression "saved to serve" may have become a cliché, but it expresses accurately the mission of every believer. The design of God's plan of world redemption is to provide salvation for all persons who choose to trust Jesus and to commission each saved person to live a life of witness and ministry.

Ministry does not end as age advances. Today God is calling grandparents to be ministers of His divine love to the family.

MINISTRY TO THE FAMILY

A little grandson pleaded with his grandma, "Don't go on a diet! I love to hug you 'cause you're fluffy!" Think of yourself as that mature sheep in the center of the family flock: the one with the rich, thick, fluffy coat of grace, wisdom, joy, and love for the lambs.

Godly grandparents like Grandma Burch love and lead the lambs of the family flock by serving. We are given a biblical model for servant leadership in the family in Luke 22:26–27, where Jesus tells us that divine love is service, not sentiment.

Yes, we love our families. But our commitment is to Christlike love, a love that serves others. These are just a few of the ways grandparents show Christlike love to family members:

- ❖ *Loving the unlovely:* the adult child who makes bad choices, the grandchild who misbehaves, the one who dresses funny, the family member who destroys your property.
- ❖ *Showing kindness:* expressing admiration, applauding accomplishments, honoring choices, encouraging new beginnings, sharing, gentleness.
- ❖ *Helpfulness:* being available when needed, standing with or standing up for a family member, advising, counseling, providing, caring.

There are more: *praying, teaching, witnessing, evangelizing, comforting.* I'm sure many others come to mind as you think about your own personal ministry to your family.

Here are two helpful tools for ministry to the family:

A Good Sense of Humor. The most successful grandparents see the best in everything and everyone. They can find the joy in any family circumstance and have the ability to laugh at themselves. It's true. A good sense of humor can come in mighty handy.

Creativity. By sharing skills such as crafts, woodworking, painting, and gardening, grandparents bless the whole family. Teaching by showing and doing passes on creative ideas to the generations. Preserving family traditions creatively and finding new ways to be a close, loving family work together toward the goal of ministry.

Remember: *The flower of ministry to the family has its roots in Christlike servanthood.*

HAZARDS TO MINISTRY TO THE FAMILY

I know we don't like to think about it. But if any of the following has happened to you, you know there are things to avoid when ministering to the family.

Overinvolvement. Exceeding ministry boundaries perhaps to the detriment of other areas of your life or causing unnecessary bad feelings.

Stress/Health Problems. Trying to do too much for too many can raise your blood pressure and your doctor bill.

Being Taken Advantage Of. Saying yes every time and allowing family members past your boundaries of time, energy, space, and money.

Rejection. Ouch! What did I do to deserve *that?* Own the problem, whatever it is, get to the bottom of it, and then take steps to resolve it.

MINISTRY TO THE CHURCH

God is calling grandparents to be ministers to the church. A new vision is sweeping the church nationwide as senior adults answer God's call to meet the needs of others. This exciting wave of Christian service takes many forms:

Teaching God's Word	Grief partner
Evangelistic visitation	Meals on Wheels delivery
Assisting voters	Telephone prayer ministry
Providing transportation	Short Term Mission Service
Janitorial help	Accounting services
Prayer partner	Teaching crafts
Visiting nursing nomes	Cooking
Reading for the sightless	Signing for the hearing-impaired
Volunteering in church office	Gardening/Mowing
Visiting the homebound	Adopting a grandchild
Car maintenance	Mentoring
Umpiring	Child care

I encourage you to join this exciting wave of ministry in your grandparenting season by using your gifts and energy in church activities that fit your schedule and abilities. By God's grace, you can make a difference!

HAZARDS TO MINISTRY TO THE CHURCH

Even in ministry to the church, we find potential hazards. Examine each individually. I hope none are familiar.

Lack of self-confidence	Knowing when to say no
Knowing when to say yes	Pride
Personality conflicts	Lack of respect for leadership

MINISTRY TO THE COMMUNITY

God is calling grandparents to be ministers of His divine love in the community. An unforgettable example of a grandparent who answered this call was Ray Smith. Ray broke his back in a fall. He lived nineteen years in a Christian nursing home, where it took 127 nursing procedures just to get him ready for the day. Ray was confined to a wheelchair, able to move only his hands and forearms. His neck fused, he looked permanently up. He said that made it easy for God to get his attention. Special prism glasses allowed him to read what his hands held. Rather than give in to his disabilities, Ray Smith accomplished more with his nineteen years than many of us do in a lifetime. He used to say, "Living is 90 percent mental, 10 percent physical, and 100 percent caring." Ray cared about his community.

❖ He spent his days duplicating tapes of the great hymns which were then sold to benefit missions.

❖ He tirelessly lobbied the state legislature for increased wages and other benefits for nursing assistants and won. Following each victory, his shout, "Praise the Lord!" reverberated in the great hall.

❖ He testified before legislative committees, saving threatened medical benefits for residents.

❖ He won many awards, including the Governor's "Volunteer of the Year" award.

❖ He witnessed to thousands and brought countless numbers of people to the saving knowledge of Jesus Christ.

Ray Smith's favorite Scripture was 2 Corinthians 4:16: "Therefore, we do not lose heart. Though outwardly we are wasting away, yet inwardly we are being renewed day by day." He was never too handicapped to reach out to his community in Christian love. He was never too old to be useful in the kingdom. Ray Smith left a legacy for all of us to think about.

There are so many ways you and I can minister to the community in which we live. Here are a few.

Nursing home volunteer	Legislative Aide
Hospital volunteer	Voting booth assistant
Public officeholder	Adopt a park
Teacher's aide	Crisis line counselor
Adopt a grandchild	Foster grandparenting

Perhaps you will think of other services you might provide that will allow your light to shine in a dark world as you minister to the people of your home area.

HAZARDS TO MINISTRY IN THE COMMUNITY

Volunteering for the community can become a full-time job. Working for the people's good is very rewarding, but some of the same potential hazards are inherent in community service.

Health problems	Age
Saying no	Burnout
Not delegating	Personality conflicts
Family obligations	Pride
Finances	Problems communicating

On the page following is a chart illustrating two lifetimes of service. It demonstrates the ways Jesus serves us and His motivation for doing so. Fill in the blanks and you will discover how your service to others compares with that of the Master.

"He went around doing good" (Acts 10:38) is a summary description of Jesus' life. What would your life description be? Many doors of ministry are open to grandparents within the family, the church, and the community. By God's grace, you can walk through them to a new life of service to others. Do what you can when you can. It could change your life!

GRACE PRINCIPLE:

God's grace is unconditional.

But to each one of us grace has been given as Christ apportioned it.

— Ephesians 4:7

Parts 4 and 5 deal with heart-touching issues facing grandparents. Before going on, take a moment to thank God for His grace, and ask Him to prepare your heart for what you are about to read.

č

Two Lifetimes of Service

Jesus Gives	By	His Motivation	I Give	By	My Motivation
Salvation	Being the Way	Salvation of our souls	Of myself		
Intimacy with God	The Holy Spirit	That we know Him intimately	Love		
Friendship	Prayer	To have fellowship with us	Counsel		
Mercy	Intercession with the Father	That we show His mercy to others	Leadership		
Willpower	Giving us choices	That we may seek His will	Understanding		
Knowledge	Speaking through the Word	That we may be instructed	Responsibility		
Joy	Answered prayer	Our happiness	Forgiveness		
Perseverance	Encouraging us	That we may not lose hope	Hope		
Forgiveness	His sacrifice	Reconciliation	Encouragement		
Strength	Reassurance	To enable us to finish the race	Joy		
Wisdom	Understanding	Growth	Caring		
Deliverance	Repentance	To set us free from bondage	Commitment		
Discipline	Testing	To build us up	Self-Esteem		
Values	His example	That we seek excellence	Knowledge		
Leadership	Showing the way	That we may lead others	Discipline		
Love	Unconditionally loving us	That we may know God's love	Honesty		
Promises	His Word	To sustain our faith	Courage		
Freedom	Redemption	That we may live as Christian's	Prayer		
Peace	Confidence in Him	That our hearts not be troubled	Of my worldly goods		
New Life	His death on the cross	That we may have eternal life	An eternal legacy		

TRYING TIMES

She was a pretty lady, sitting in the back row of one hundred or so attending a weekend grandparenting seminar. On the last day she came forward to say thank you. She smiled and said softly, "My husband and I just buried our daughter after watching her battle cancer for eight months. Her only child, our six-year-old grandson, now lives with us. Our adopted thirty-year-old son has AIDS and is dying in the back bedroom of our home. His homosexual friends come in and out, and we do our best to answer our grandson's questions."

"How can you smile through such tragic circumstances?" I asked.

She answered, "My God told me He will never give me more than I can bear and that He will never leave me or forsake me. Knowing that, I am filled with gratitude for His goodness to me!"

Contemporary grandparents who are facing horrific challenges such as these, cry out, "Abba, Father!" And our gracious God is faithful to meet every need at the trying times.

e

Chapter 13

DIVORCE
AND REMARRIAGE

It had been a wonderful "Gramma time" together, a whole day of stories, games, good food, and hugs. Now it was bedtime. My 6-year-old granddaughter, Michelle, jumped into her "Gramma bed" fresh from a bubble bath with rubber and plastic friends. She bowed her head to ask a blessing for everyone, including the cat. Walking into the room to say goodnight, I overheard her close her prayer softly, "And dear God, if you decide you need my grandma in heaven, please ask me about it first. Amen!" With my heart almost bursting with grandparent love, I wanted to protect Michelle from all harm, to stand alongside her on the road of life, and hand-deliver her to maturity without a single scar.

Then came the divorce. Shortly after her parents announced they were splitting up, Michelle and I were making cookies in my kitchen. In the middle of one teaspoon of this and one tablespoon of that, Michelle's eyes locked on mine. She said, "My daddy only comes home every other weekend now, Gramma. Is that okay?" *How do you answer questions from a grandchild of divorce?*

Our four-year-old grandson, Samuel, sat nervously between his father and mother at a psychological evaluation ordered by the family court in their divorce. The doctor sitting behind the desk asked Samuel how he felt about his parents' divorce. Samuel said he was going to "fix it so they could be together." The doctor leaned forward and asked Samuel, "How are you going to do that, Sam?" My grandson's face lighted up with hope. He puffed two breaths in and out as he looked up at his mother, then his father, then back at the doctor who was waiting for an answer. Suddenly, all of the excitement drained from his freckled face. He jumped down from the chair, ran over to the psychologist's couch, rolled up in the fetal position facing the wall, and wailed, "I don't know!" *How can a grandparent cope with the personal pain we know our grandchildren endure when their parents divorce?*

Divorce is the biggest problem facing Christian grandparents today. Four of our seven children's marriages have ended in divorce, affecting six of our twelve perfect grandchildren. I have listened to countless grandparents pour out their personal anguish over the circumstances and repercussions of children's divorces and the effect on their grandchildren. It has been confirmed for me that the key to grandparenting by grace in these tragic cases is to *let the parents focus on their troubles. You focus on the grandchild.*

Once again, we have no control over what parents will do. There is little if anything grandparents can do except pray for quick resolution of the problems and for any possible reconciliation. This is not to say we ignore the parents or do not give counsel to them when appropriate. But our concentration should be on the grandchildren. We remain the grandparent. Our job is to comfort, protect, and pray for the whole family and be there when they need us.

ANSWERING THE HARD QUESTIONS

When Michelle asked me that question, I silently asked God to give me the right words. I reached across the kitchen counter, put my hands on hers, and looked into her searching eyes. Only God gave me the words, "Michelle, your daddy loves you very much. Your mommy loves you very much. And Grampa and I love you very much!" Michelle smiled and went back to the recipe. She didn't need an "answer." She needed to unload some of her fear, confusion, and hurt. There were many things I might have said; but by the grace of God, I did not say them.

It would have been wrong to answer her question with a yes or a no, for such an answer would have been opinion. It is not a grandparent's right to express opinions to a grandchild of divorce. Our duty is to respond with love and understanding, allowing the child to vent emotions that may have been stifled for some time. Responding with a question is good. "How do you feel about it? Would you like to talk about it?"

Further explanation from a grandparent will only confuse the child. You see, a grandchild of divorce stands between two people he or she deeply loves. Siding with one parent against the other might be easy to do, especially if *our* child has been wronged in some way. But if we do that, we damage or destroy the trust of the child. "If I say anything good about my daddy, Grandma will be mad." "If I say anything good about my mommy, Grandpa will be mad, so I won't say anything at all."

Some grandparents have crossed the line in situations like this, blurted out their own ideas, and now the child doesn't feel safe to share feelings and fears.

If something like this ever happens to you,

❖ Answer the question with a question.
❖ Be sincere and loving.
❖ Be brief.
❖ Allow the child to unload feelings and fears, knowing they are safe with you.
❖ Keep confidences.

Psychologists tell us that children of divorce feel responsible for the divorce. "If I'd made my bed like my mom said, she'd still be here." "If I'd been a better kid, my dad wouldn't have left."

Often, by asking questions, grandchildren of divorce are just searching for something that will say they didn't cause it after all. We can help by reassuring the child, valuing the child, building self-esteem, and keeping an unbiased attitude.

More Questions
from Grandchildren of Divorce

Similar responses apply to other more serious and complicated questions asked of grandparents by grandchildren of divorce:

1. Who will take care of me now?
2. Where is my dad/mom living now?
3. Are my parents crazy?
4. Will my dad/mom get sick, hit by a car, or worse?
5. Will we have enough money now?
6. Will I have to change schools?
7. Will Mom/Dad marry someone else? Will they keep me?
8. Will somebody take Mom's/Dad's place? Will they like me?
9. Does my dad/mom still love me?
10. Do you still love me?

A grandparent's loving response to a grandchild of divorce can help maintain an ongoing, loving relationship.

Coping with Divorce

Here are coping mechanisms that worked for me as I vowed to grandparent by grace and help my grandchildren in crisis.

1. Pray without ceasing. Pray for the protection of innocent grandchildren. Pray for reconciliation.
2. Before, during, and after the divorce, let the parents focus on their troubles while you focus on the grandchild.
3. Offer to take your grandchild to age-appropriate Christian events. You may be the only one who does.

4. Use the parent's explanation of the divorce as the basis for answering any questions from the child.
5. Listen. Don't rush in to "fix it" as little Samuel wanted so desperately to do. Keep your grandchild's confidence.
6. Affirm your grandchild often.
7. Never speak against either parent.
8. Understand mood changes. Your grandchild's world has cracked at the foundation, and everything is unstable.
9. Play with your grandchild. Laugh. Have fun together.
10. Keep your normal routine at home when the child comes to visit. You represent stability in a chaotic world.
11. Be available to babysit, especially if the grandchild would have to spend that time alone at home.
12. Assure your grandchild of your love often. Hugs are excellent therapy for grandchildren of divorce.
13. Join or start a support group for grandparents of divorce.
14. Take care of your health. Body defenses break down without proper nutrition, rest, exercise, and relaxation.
15. When couples divide, let your love multiply.

Hatred stirs up dissension, but love covers over all wrongs.
— Proverbs 10:12

Too Much Caring

A lady, we'll call her Lilly, asked to speak to me after a workshop last fall. She tearfully poured out the fact that on her way to the retreat, her husband of thirty-nine years said he was going to leave her because she was "too tied up in the kid's problems." For nine years, she tried to make life easier for her daughter, son-in-law, and three grandchildren. The couple had separated twice. Lilly was so emotionally involved in the details of the separations and the divorce, paid little attention to her husband. He had taken a backseat to the kids' troubles, and he was fed up.

Later that evening, Lilly went back to her room, put her arms around her mate, and told him that when they got home, things would be different. She apologized for the mistakes she had made and promised not to allow herself to be so heavily involved in the kids' lives' anymore. They talked at length about their feelings, reminiscing about all the good years God had given them together and the blessings they had shared.

The next morning at breakfast, I heard my name being called across the cafeteria. It was Lilly, smiling broadly and saying with great joy, "My marriage is saved!"

Bringing Them Back Home

In Isaiah 25:4, the prophet praises the Lord: "You have been a refuge for the poor, a refuge for the needy in his distress, a shelter from the storm and a shade from the heat." We can be a Christ-centered refuge for children and grandchildren of divorce. Difficulties come into play, however, when clear guidelines are not set at the beginning of the stay.

The same principles used in dealing with money issues apply here: pray, plan, and partner.

Pray. Before allowing or asking an adult child with one or more of your grandchildren to move into your house, pray about it. Ask God if this is His will in the matter, and take time to discern what it is He would have you do. Do not act hastily.

Plan. If you just open your door and your arms, you risk becoming a parent to everybody over time. Make a plan. Make clear that this is a temporary situation until he or she can resume the responsibility of raising your grandchild(ren).

Partner. Insist that the plan agreed to is adhered to. Do your part, in every instance showing love and understanding. But do not allow the adult child to break the covenant and take advantage of you. Be flexible but firm. Allow your child to suffer the consequences of his or her actions. Partnering also includes honoring their choice should they decide not to come home. To some, such a choice would signify further failure. They may want to make new lives on their own.

WHEN YOUR CHILD REMARRIES

Remarriage can bring blessed stability to a child's life. A healthy second marriage can also be an opportunity for a grandchild to have a renewed sense of security and belonging. Loving grandparents can play an important role in this process.

Here are some questions asked by grandparents.

❖ *What kind of stepparent will the new person be?* This is an important question in light of horrific abuse statistics. If you know the person before the marriage and danger signals appear, speak up. You have a right to ask questions of those entrusted with the future of your grandchild(ren).

❖ *Will my grandchild(ren) like the new stepmom or stepdad?* Counselors say that kids of divorce are hungry for the absent parent's affection and can expect more than is reasonable from the new parent. Such a child is vulnerable to a false sense of security that can lead to disappointment and emotional trauma. Godly grandparents can encourage the child to be patient and understanding. We also make excellent listening ports in a storm.

❖ *Will the new couple have enough money to adequately care for the grandchildren?* That's their problem, not yours. Remember, you are not in control of that family. Besides, if they do need money, you'll probably be the first to know it. (Write the principles of giving and loaning money from chapter 4 on your "doorposts"!)

❖ *Will the newcomer care about my grandchild(ren)?* Be alert. Be involved in your grandchild's life. Eighty percent of divorced women in America remarry at least once, leaving millions of children in emotional confusion. Let your grandchild see you as an example of consistency.

❖ *Will I like the children being brought into this marriage? Will they call me "Grandma," and is that all right?* Every new family will be different. Children brought into the new family are a challenge for every member of the existing family. Just remember that nowhere is it written that you have to like them! You probably will. Maybe you won't. God will give you grace to deal with it. Show your grandparent love, and see what happens.

❖ *Will the newcomer nurture the faith of my grandchild(ren)?* Sometimes church, family devotions, and prayer decline when a couple is busy building a new life together with ready-made children. You can stand in the gap as a Christlike example, helping to keep your grandchild's faith strong and growing.

❖ *How will my relationship with my grandchild(ren) change?* When a divorced child remarries, your relationship with your grandchild may indeed change. Grandparents might be drawn closer into the family. Or you might find yourselves feeling outside the circle, less a part of the new family than of the old. Be patient. Their agenda is full.

<u>GRACE PRINCIPLE:</u>

Future generations need God's grace.

For this reason I remind you to fan into flame the gift of God, which is in you . . . . For God did not give us a spirit of timidity, but a spirit of power, of love and of self-discipline.

— 2 Timothy 1:6–7

Divorce and remarriage can bring about change, both good and bad. Change impacts how others view us and how we view ourselves, as we will see next.

ॐ

Chapter 14

OTHER CHANGING RELATIONSHIPS

Change is inevitable. Children grow up. They don't always make us happy by what they do or have to do. They may go away and leave us missing them. Or *we* move away to a better climate in retirement. Our lives change dramatically with loss and maybe even another marriage. We might find ourselves grandparenting someone else's grandchildren or having several generations living under one roof.

How we respond to these and other changes in our grandparenting season can make or break our relationships with those we love.

LONG-DISTANCE GRANDPARENTING

Jeanine and Al lived three blocks from their grandchildren: Jenny, fifteen, Jason, nine, and James Albert, four. Attending church and dinners were family affairs. Summers were great fun, especially when Grandpa Al umpired the neighborhood ballgames or everybody piled into the motor home for a fishing trip.

The Christmas parade and Fourth of July fireworks were traditional times for this close-knit family. Jeanine babysat

James Albert weekday mornings so his mother could work part-time. Jason and Jenny stopped by for a few minutes on their way home from school almost every day.

"We knew there might someday come a time when our son-in-law would be transferred in his job," Jeanine remembers. "But when it actually happened, it was like somebody yanked out my heart. We held up pretty well before they left. After they moved, Al and I missed the kids so badly. It was hard for them, too. We caused quite a phone bill and decided we'd better get creative."

One of the things Jeanine missed most was poring over her Sunday sermon notes with her teenage granddaughter Jenny when she stopped by during the week. It had become a treasured time for both of them. So Jeanine decided to have a Bible study by mail with Jenny.

Each Monday, she mails her Sunday sermon notes to her granddaughter. Jenny mails hers to her grandmother, usually with her unique comments and a "happy face" drawn in the corner. "It's as close to being with her as I can get," says Jeanine. "The long-distance sharing of our faith is building a very special bond between us. It is exciting in every way!"

Grandpa Al is planning for them to travel by motor home to visit the young family next summer. Grandma Jeanine writes her grandsons twice a month, telling them news from their old neighborhood. She includes stamped, addressed envelopes so the boys can respond. One day she opened one of those envelopes to find a tiny, dead grasshopper James Albert wanted her to have. "Listen, I don't mind!" says Grandma. "I'll take anything I get. That means he loves me! The only problem is that when I get something like that, I don't know whether to laugh or cry. See, I still miss him something terrible!"

Yes, it hurts. But Jeanine and Al are making the best of it and reaping dividends in their loving relationship with their grandchildren. Change does not have to be negative. It all depends on what we do with it.

Here are some other ideas for grandparenting long-distance.

- Call them every Sunday morning. Then go to church and pray for the child.
- For young grandchildren, write an original story of three or four paragraphs, glue it to colored paper, and mail it to them. Children love to receive mail.
- Send books to elementary-aged grandchildren.
- Write letters about things that happen at your house: squirrels stashing their food under the tree stump, raccoons thumping onto the roof, birds singing in the feeder.
- Have your spouse videotape you reading a bedtime story. Send the tape and the book. Mom sends the tape back to you for another story! (You probably won't get it back. Your grandchild will show it to friends and want to see it over and over again.)
- Make audio tapes of events at your house and mail them. Listening to the tape makes the child feel part of your everyday life.
- Take a grandchild's address with you when traveling. Buy a postcard from that area, address it, and write, "I saw this today and thought of you."
- Keep a scrapbook of events you can show your grandchildren the next time you see them.
- Keep stamps from your mail, and then send them to your grandchild to start a collection.
- Send an inexpensive gift—a bookmark or stickers on a day other than a birthday or holiday that says "I love you." Posters are a hit and mail easily in cardboard tubes.
- Avoid sending money for birthdays or at Christmas unless the parent approves.
- Plan your visit to grandchildren or their visit to you by mail and phone. Allow the children to be part of the planning excitement.

❖ If you have a modem on your computer at work or at home, buy one for your long-distance grandchildren and keep in touch.

The whole idea of serious long-distance grandparenting is that the link not be broken. Never let a generation miss out on you and the unique difference you can make in their lives, especially with all of the changes happening for grandchildren of divorce or remarriage. As one little fellow put it, "When I get to feeling sad and lonely, at least I know my Grandma is out there, waiting for me to come over."

STEP-GRANDPARENTS

It's a huge change when we inherit grandchildren through the remarriage of our adult child. Helenka's son, Gerard, had given her two "perfect" grandchildren. Now he was married for the second time to a woman with two children of her own. "Does that mean I have four grandchildren now? I don't know how to act," she told me. "What if they call me Grandma? Is that OK with their mother? Besides, I don't even know these children!"

They don't know you either. Grandparents are far better off not pretending. Children know when adults put on an act. It's best to let the relationship develop naturally. Be yourself. Believe me, the children will be themselves and let you know how they feel.

Save yourself a lot of grief. Don't try to pretend you love or even like the new kids. Give it time. Be honest about your feelings and let God work on the relationship. All of us grandparents who have had our lives enriched by precious step-grandchildren say, "Amen."

Helenka had some clear choices. She could either avoid the new "grandchildren," or she could adopt a positive attitude and make an attempt to get to know them. She chose the latter and has never regretted it.

The circumstances surrounding these "new families" can be devastating for grandparents. Our grandchild's parent may choose to marry an unbeliever. Sometimes "damaged kids" become our step-grandchildren. That's what happened to Ann.

Ann raised her son, Philip, in a Christian home. Philip excelled in engineering and had a good job. Now he was living with a woman and her small son from an abusive first marriage. Ann had no control over the situation and didn't quite know how to feel when she heard that the marriage had taken place.

On a Sunday afternoon, Philip, his wife, and her seven-year-old son came to visit. Ann prayed for grace in this experience. She loved her son and, like all parents, wanted the best for her child. The door opened, and there they were! Ann did her best through the awkward introductions. She noticed that the boy, Nathan, blond and small for his age, looked down, holding on tight to his mother's hand.

After a dinner during which Philip did most of the talking, Nathan seemed to have relaxed a bit. He surprised everyone by asking Ann if he could go out in the backyard. The new step-grandmother, of course, said, "Certainly."

Nathan's hand slipped rather naturally into hers. Once outside, the boy bolted across the grass, running at full speed from the fence to the tree to the flower garden and back to Ann, falling deliriously into her arms. Stunned, Ann looked down into Nathan's suddenly radiant face. Her defenses melted away when he said to her, "I've never had a backyard."

He had never had a grandmother either. Innocent children like Nathan are starving for affection and deserving of unbiased grandparent love and attention. Neither we nor the children can control what parents will do. We're in the same boat. Therefore, much more is accomplished when we concentrate not on how this blessing came to be but on the child's best interests.

Step-grandparenting is a ministry. We are called to put God's love into action. We do that best when we focus on the child. Focusing our attention on children can also help when changes occur in our own lives as senior adults.

SEVERAL GENERATIONS UNDER ONE ROOF

Remember the Waltons on television? Grandma and Grandpa Walton lived with their son and daughter-in-law and seven grandchildren in a house filled with Christian love and sharing. Theirs was a healthy family experiencing the joys and trials of growing together. Several generations under one roof was not unusual in the thirties and forties. In fact, it was simply understood that in times of need, family members reached out to to help each other. It was the right thing to do.

It's still the right thing to do, except that millions of today's multi-generational households bear no resemblance to the Walton clan. Instead of Grandma and Grandpa, Mom and Dad, and the kids living in bliss and harmony, it's *Grandma's* house with her elderly parents, her divorced daughter, and the grandchildren. Or it's Grandma and Grandpa taking in *both* a son and a daughter with any number of their young children. Or it's Grandma raising the grandchildren alone, coping with the disastrous effects of an adult child's life choices.

There are names for these conglomerate families, the "Sandwich Generation" or "Skip Generation Families." Almost all suffer from financial, psychological, spiritual, and emotional stress, as you will see in part 5 of this book. Those who can meet the needs of these families will be on the cutting edge of ministry in the nineties.

Going back home with the kids can be one of the toughest decisions a parent has to make. This is particularly true after a long struggle for independence doesn't work out. Loving grandparents offer a welcome haven, a chance to formulate a new plan and to regroup emotionally. Relationally, though, it can be rough living under the same roof with adult children who overstep their boundaries or leave the raising of the children to Grandma and Grandpa. Clear communication between all parties plus sticking to the plan are always the keys to success when two or more generations live together.

FOSTER GRANDPARENTING

Ruth Moore of Archer City, Texas, grew up as the youngest of eight children on a "poor farm." Saved at the age of ten, she found whatever work she could do through the Depression and World War II. Ruth Moore has spent her entire life in service to her family, her church, and her community. She has taught Sunday School lessons at a local nursing home for fifteen years.

In 1988, Ruth was caring for an older sister and raising two grandchildren in her home in addition to helping out wherever she was needed in the community. She had plenty on her plate, but there was a stirring in her spirit that could not be ignored. The breakdown of the family and the plight of America's children, especially disabled and disadvantaged children, touched her deeply. Ruth reached out to help.

Ruth became a foster grandparent in November 1988 under a government program signed into law in 1965 by President Lyndon Johnson as part of the Older Americans Act. The program was designed for older adults to supplement their income by caring for handicapped children. The original "granny" of the group was Dacy Briggs, loved and admired by everyone involved in the program, who is now eighty years old and living in Wichita Falls.

According to Ruth, the Foster Grandparent Program in Archer City is one of the few working in conjunction with the public school system.

"Our supervisors have to drive over one hundred miles to check on us to make sure we are following guidelines. We are paid just a stipend, but it is nontaxable. The real pay is in the work. Most of the kids are from dysfunctional homes. I have worked with three children since they were three. One is now in kindergarten, one in first grade, and one in third grade. The third grader's mother is in prison for murder. The youngest boy has cerebral palsy. He is a beautiful child, and he has already mastered the art of manipulation. These children are hyperactive and slow learners. The little girl talks a mile a minute and is very thin from eating junk food most of her life. Two other 'grandchildren' are preschoolers. One has a speech defect but has made tremendous progress.

"My job as a foster grandparent is to give these children love, personal attention, and total acceptance and to teach them good manners and proper actions with their peers. It is so rewarding to have them wave to me and call, 'Hi, Granny!'"

"Raising my own grandchildren has been a joy as I have been able to provide care and nurturing for them. I receive the same blessings as a foster grandparent. Children are children. They all need love. I thank God every day for the energy to make a contribution in these youngsters' lives."

(Unfortunately, not all foster grandparenting programs run as smoothly as this one.)

ADOPT-A-GRANDCHILD PROGRAMS

Fragmented intergenerational relationships prompt more and more young parents today to say, "We would give almost anything we own for a genuine grandparent for our child." These parents miss the influence of godly grandparents for a variety of reasons.

Distance. The real grandparents live in another state, another country.

Loss. The real grandparents have died.

Attitude. The real grandparents don't care.

Young people need older people to talk to, play with, hug, listen to, giggle with, and be silly with. Children need to learn from the vast storehouse of wisdom and life experiences of older people. Statistics on divorce and other tragedies highlight the great needs of children for healthy role models.

On the other hand, there are thousands of senior adults who may have no natural grandchildren and are missing out on the joys of grandparenting. Perhaps they are even longing for a loving relationship with a child. How can they find each other?

Adoption! Oh, not formal adoption, of course. Nothing written, except on the heart. This kind of adoption is the nurturing of a loving relationship with one special child for that child's lifetime as a "Grandma" or a "Grandpa." If you decide to do this:

❖ Make no promises. Let the relationship develop naturally, always remembering that the parent has ultimate control.

❖ Keep an open line of communication with the parent(s).

❖ Be honest about what you can and cannot do in all areas.

❖ Make no written agreements.

What Do "Adopted Grandparents" Do?

❖ Have special times with the child at a time and place scheduled by the child's parent(s) and Sunday dinner as often as fits the family's lifestyle.

❖ Be available as a "safety net" for the parents, especially if both parents work and/or the child is latchkey.

❖ Join the family for holiday and birthday celebrations, giving and receiving small "Grandma" and/or "Grandpa" gifts. "Adopted" grandparents are included in every major event in the home just as a natural grandparent would be.

❖ "Adopted Grandpas" can fill a crucial gap as a trusted, wise and caring male role model for the child of a single mom.

Perhaps there is a potential "grandchild" in your neighborhood or in your church. If your church does not have an "Adopt-a-Grandchild" program, why not start one?

My friend, Josie, who is sixty-seven, teaches Sunday School. There she bonded with one of her students, five-year-old Kaitlin, whose grandmother had died. Kaitlin's parents knew the relationship had blossomed over time into a warm, loving one and asked Josie if their family might "adopt" her as grandmother to their little girl and her brother. Josie happily agreed. "Grandma Josie," a widow with no grandchildren, loves Kaitlin and her brother, Aaron, as if they were her own. She prays for them daily and has dinner with the Jensens every other Sunday. There is always time after dinner to read to the children or to tell stories about her many years as a medical missionary. Josie attends special holiday times with the family and is thrilled with her title of "Grandma." She is putting a little extra love, laughter, and joy into two children's lives, saying, "I haven't replaced anyone. I just plain love them, and they know it. The truth is, I am the one who is blessed!"

GRANDPARENTS WHO MARRY AGAIN

Years after my dad's death, Mom was sometimes asked why she didn't marry again. She always responded the same way, "Why should I? I had the best for fifty years!"

Some of us feel that way, and that's fine. Other grandparents who have lost a spouse can find a new life when they remarry: a companion with like interests such as travel, hobbies, or church or community service.

Grandparents who marry again need to pay particular attention to the feelings of those dear family members who have been an integral part of their lives. Adult children can be thrilled or upset. It all depends on how the news is handled. For example, how should the "new grandpa" or "new grandma" be introduced to the children and grandchildren?

"My kids weren't really sure what to think of my new marriage after John passed away," Marion confided. "I made sure I told them about Thurgood early on and made lots of opportunities for family to meet him. 'Goody's' robust personality made him an almost instant hit with the whole family. Before long, the grandkids were calling him 'Grandpa Goody'! He loves that because he doesn't have any grandchildren of his own."

Good rules of thumb for introducing the new person to grandchildren are:

1. Bring the new person into your grandchild's life as early in your courtship as possible.
2. Be patient. Let the relationship develop naturally.
3. Bring any problems that arise to the Lord in prayer, and talk openly about them with your partner and members of the family.

When grandparents fall out of love, however, and break their marriage commitment made before God, the scenario is very different. Family relationships can fall like dominos. Children, grandchildren, and all family members are adversely affected. Their shock, humiliation, anger, or grief at the divorce can lead to rejection of the new person when Grandma or Grandpa remarries.

Vernon divorced Katherine after thirty-seven years of marriage, six children, and fourteen grandchildren. Within a year, he was married again—to Katherine's lifelong friend, Betty. Both Vernon and Betty were effectively shunned by the family. This is serious business when we consider how many grandchildren lost the important bond with their grandfather.

Complications arise even when the new step-grandparent is accepted by the family. For example, grandchildren remember the first one emotionally, if not verbally. Much time, energy, and patience is necessary for a smooth transition on both sides. It's worth the effort because children need all the love they can get, and everybody knows that one *can't* have too many grandchildren. We need each other.

Widowed Grandparents

Loss of a life mate can bring pain that defies description for the surviving spouse. Six months after losing her husband, Roberta received an invitation to come to a meeting at a singles social club. Outraged, she screamed into the telephone, "I'm not single! I've been married for forty-one years!"

For a couple with a long history together, grandparenting has been a shared experience. Now everything is different. You are left to carry on alone. Here are survival suggestions to help the widowed grandparent.

1. Don't allow your pain to diminish your participation in the lives of your family. Keep your grandparenting relationships strong.
2. Allow family and friends to share your grief. They need to.
3. Depend on God's promises in the Bible. Spend much time being strengthened and comforted by the Word. Read daily, if not hourly.
4. Share your concerns about the future with a trusted confidant in the family.
5. As soon as you can, get busy doing something good for someone else.
6. Talk with your grandchildren often about the good times of the past. Talk to anyone who will listen. Talk to yourself. Talk to God.
7. A real life, beyond mere survival, depends upon the heart of the survivor. Even if your heart feels broken, it can still give and receive love.

On the next page are the words of a communion hymn written by John Wesley. I have added a line between each of the writer's lines to personalize the hymn as an encouragement to all who have lost a mate.

Our needy souls sustain
the loss
With fresh supplies of love,
from friends and family
Till all thy life we gain,
as my dear (name)_____ has gained
And all thy fullness prove,
I will behold thy promises
And, strengthened by thy perfect grace,
I will
Behold without a veil thy face.
and stand in Your glory. Amen.

GRACE PRINCIPLE:

We will always need God's grace.

But he gives us more grace. That is why Scripture says: "God opposes the proud but gives grace to the humble."

— James 4:6

The next chapter includes true stories of grandparents who have walked through or are walking through the dark valleys of a grandchild's death. I pray God will give you His peace if you personally identify with any of these stories.

ॐ

Chapter 15

GRANDPARENTS COPING WITH LOSS

Grandparents go through many trials in a lifetime. The valleys are as much a part of the job as the mountaintops. Christians know that; and we trust God as we walk through valleys, leaning on His strength, drawing on His wisdom and His sustaining grace. Following are testimonies from grandparents who have made the ultimate sacrifice, that of giving up a grandchild to His divine plan. You will see clearly how God's grace is manifested in each case.

DRUNK DRIVING

On March 4, 1982, Barbara and Marvin Norris were driving in their Volkswagen. Glancing at the rearview mirror, Marvin saw a car roaring toward them at a high rate of speed. He cried out to his wife, "He's going to hit us!" Barbara tells the story.

> There was no time to react. The car smashed into ours at ninety miles per hour, sending us up into the air, then crashing to the pavement, rolling over and over and over, we don't know how many times. We came to a stop, our car crunched to half its normal length. Inside in the eerie silence, I saw Marvin, horribly cut and bruised. He moved.

He began to gently stroke my head, which lay against his thigh. "Be still. Be still," he said quietly between barely audible prayers for help to come.

The first face we saw was a deputy sheriff who goes to our church. What a blessing! It was so good to see a familiar face! He talked to us until medical help arrived, telling us of a second blessing—that after such a bad crash, it was most unusual for the two of us to end up close together to comfort one another and not to be thrown from the car.

My injuries were multiple, including several broken vertebrae. My leg was smashed flat. It is deformed now, but I can walk. Praise God!

We spent many long months in the hospital and in therapy. The offending driver was a forty-nine-year-old alcoholic whose mother paid the fine. He was in jail an hour and a half and got out on personal recognizance.

Nine years later, on March 16, 1991, we had just enjoyed a wonderful day with our grandson, Brady, age ten. Our family credits Brady with getting his grandfather and me through rehabilitation after the crash in 1982. A bright, loving, and compassionate boy and the light of my life, Brady was just a year or so old when the crash occurred but spent long hours listening to me, sitting with me, insisting on staying by my side, looking at storybooks and loving me during recuperation from my injuries. I felt I could conquer anything with Brady's love. I know he is the reason I can walk today.

His mother, Cindy, picked Brady up that day in March 1991. She and Stevie Lynn, our little granddaughter, went later to do some shopping, while Brady went with his dad to his job. Brady liked to ride on the motorcycle behind his dad. On the way home, a pickup truck coming toward them swerved, then overcorrected and plowed into Steve's motorcycle. Our son died instantly. Brady lived almost an hour. The only concern the young drunk driver of the pickup truck voiced was how much damage there had been to his truck. He was sentenced to forty-eight months in prison and was out in two years. And I am left to live without my only son and my beloved grandson, Brady.

Brady. I miss his warm little body. I miss his compassion for people, the excitement he had for life and the future. He was so gifted and accomplished many good things in his brief life.

I miss my son. I have the memory of his last phone call to me after keeping Brady overnight and the last words he said to me, "I love you, Mom. I don't know what we'd ever do without you."

Drunk drivers take away so much from every member of the family affected. Even those yet unborn suffer. We have ten grandchildren, including Brady. The new ones can't understand why Grandma can't pick them up or play with them or dress up in high heels. My husband has no son to tell about the mileage he gets on his truck or to help move the couch or to fish with. My mother, eighty years of age when Steve and Brady were killed, started going downhill healthwise from the trauma. My daughters do not smile anymore.

The first drunk driver broke my bones. The second one broke my heart. A drunk driver took my physical abilities but not my mental capabilities, and never will he break me spiritually. I have forgiven both drivers. If justice wasn't done here on earth, I know the Lord will take care of it. I have to turn it over to Him. My faith has been tested. I think, *Why them and not me?* I have so many questions. I know I will have the answers some day. *Why* doesn't matter. I have to be a good example. Bitterness and anger would only cause my family pain.

Today, Barbara is coordinator for the Victim Impact Panel of MADD (Mothers Against Drunk Driving) of Cowlitz

County in Washington state, where in 1993, drunk drivers caused 328 deaths and 12,580 injuries. Nationally, alcohol-related traffic crashes are decreasing, from 26,000 in 1988 to 17,699 in 1992. According to MADD, however, a person's chances of being involved in a drunk driving crash in his lifetime is 2 in 5.[1]

Barbara wants everyone to know that drunk driving incidents are not accidents. "You don't go to prison for an accident. These are crashes and they are criminal."

Barbara found solace in writing her feelings in this poem for her daughter-in-law:

TO CINDY

I gave birth to my son and he married you.
You two became one and you gave birth to
Two of the loveliest grandchildren a grandmother could love
And now my son and your son are in heaven above.
Yes, our sons are gone and we miss them so much.
We cry in the night for just one last touch
Of Steve and Brady love.
They were stolen from us. We've all been deprived
Because of one young man's choice to drink and to drive.
When you look at Stevie, your daughter that Steve gave you
You'll know how I feel when I look at you.
'Cause you are my daughter. Steve gave me one, too.
You are my daughter, so precious you see
You are the daughter my son gave to me.

— Barbara Scott Norris

ABORTION

Abortion takes the lives of millions of unborn babies every year in America. We don't know how many. According to the National Center for Health Statistics, the number of legally induced abortions is 1.6 million, but ten of the fifty states do not survey abortion statistics.[2]

This act reverberates throughout the lifetime of the mother and the lives of extended family members, including grandparents. Often, abortion can be the result of a mother's own childhood of pain, deprivation, and mistakes. Here is Patty's story.

My two girls had difficult childhoods with an alcoholic father. I divorced him and was married again to an abusive man who I think, although I could never prove it, molested my girls. In 1980, my daughter, Elizabeth, then sixteen, became pregnant by her boyfriend. I took her to Planned Parenthood, where she was advised to get an abortion. Nothing was explained to us there. I didn't know better, so I went along with it. Her boyfriend made the arrangements. That was the first of many abortions for Elizabeth. My daughter, Jerri, now twenty-seven, has had numerous abortions as well. She also sold two other babies immediately after birth in order to finance her cocaine, alcohol, and marijuana addictions. Jerri told me that another baby died at birth. I was particularly grieved by this one because I did not believe her. I suspected that the baby did not die at birth but rather was adopted by a Canadian couple, but I could not prove it. For years I wondered if there wasn't a little grandson of mine growing up somewhere in Canada.

Five years ago I married a Christian man and asked Jesus Christ to become Lord of my life. Thoughts of the grandbaby who supposedly died at birth haunted me. One day I got the courage to go to the Bureau of Records. I remember the day well, just before Mother's Day. The record indicated the baby, Andrew, born to my daughter had indeed died with the umbilical cord wrapped around his neck. But somehow, I still didn't believe it.

As I was leaving the Bureau of Records, a strange feeling overcame me. I had to stop on the stairs. It was as though God's angels surrounded me. I don't know how I knew it, but I *knew* that baby was alive, either in heaven or on earth. It no longer mattered where. God, by His grace, gave me peace about this grandson to enable me to pray for him and for the others.

Jerri has recently given birth to two girls, my granddaughters, who live with their father. I see them often, and they give me great joy! Jerri has just completed a Narcotics Anonymous course and is working hard to get her life in order and regain custody of her daughters.

I have forgiven both of my girls for what they have done. They have forgiven me for all of the mistakes I made. Elizabeth masks her emotions. I am encouraging her to get counseling. Jerri talks of a "big black hole" she has inside that never goes away. Neither of my girls has accepted the Lord.

I am thankful for the women in my Bible study group who have listened to me, held me when I cried, and prayed for me and with me. Most of all I thank God for redeeming me. I want to be the best grandmother I can be. I write in a prayer journal about my feelings and what I have learned about my faith. I show it to my daughters often, hoping and praying they will see in its pages the depth of my love for them and for my grandchildren.

Most of all, I want my girls to see that God loves them and longs for fellowship with them before it's too late.

Gun Violence

Evelyn will always remember her granddaughter Amy's seventeenth birthday. It was October 23, 1992.

Evelyn and her husband Bertram lived six hundred miles away but would not think of missing Amy's birthday. Theirs was a close, cherished relationship that started the day Amy was born. It was Evelyn who drove Amy home from the hospital. Here is her story.

Amy and I had something special. She used to tell me her secrets. I knew what was bothering her and what made her happy. She would call me long distance just to tell me about something at school or to ask my advice about a friend's problem. When she stayed overnight, I would sit on the edge of her bed and just listen to her talk about her hopes and dreams. She loved going to church with us.

I remember every event of that seventeenth birthday celebration. We had such a good time. The morning we had to drive back home, Amy was up early, her ponytail swinging from side to side as she got ready to go to school. She leaned over and kissed me, saying, "I'm off! I'll miss you. I love you. You're the best Grandma in the whole world!"

Less than one month later she was dead, killed by a gunshot wound to the head. The news came to us by telephone from our daughter on November 21. It is all a blurred memory for me. Amy was shot while visiting her friend, Travis, along with her girlfriend. The nineteen-year-old boy brought out a stolen gun and pointed it in fun at my precious Amy's head. Amy said, "Don't do that!" And the gun went off.

The light of my life was gone. It was the blackest moment of my entire life.

We called our pastor, and he came immediately. The whole congregation family came together to pray for us. We all prayed for Travis, who showed deep remorse and repentence, that he would find the Lord through this terrible thing.

Travis, who had been in trouble before and who my daughter and her husband had befriended, was sentenced to four and a half years in jail for manslaughter. And we must cope without Amy.

I promised Amy a new car if she never drank or smoked. Instead of a new car, I bought her a funeral.

I try to be the best support I can be for my daughter and son-in-law in their grief. For weeks, my daughter awakened with agonizing screams, realizing she faced another day without Amy.

I know God is in control of our lives. He has been so good to me. As I cried out to Him in my sorrow, He quieted me and gave me these promises:

> *My grace is sufficient for you.*
> *I am with you always.*
> *I will come again and*
> *You will see Amy again.*

By the year 2003 the number of firearm-related deaths will surpass the number of motor-vehicle-related crashes, and firearms will become the leading cause of injury-related death in America. Guns kill forty children every day in America.[3] Most of them are somebody's grandchildren.

Premature Grandbaby

Heidi and Mel were expecting their first child Thanksgiving Day 1993. Gloria and Warren, Mel's parents, were overjoyed at the news, and looked forward to the due date. The telephone call from their son, Mel, on August 11 at 5:30 in the morning shattered their sleep *and* their dreams. Here is Gloria's story.

She can't be in labor at twenty-five weeks! A C-section? an emergency? How can this be? We rushed to the hospital in shock and disbelief.

There in the isolette lay our grandson, Connor, one pound, seven and one-half ounces, twelve and one-half inches long. So perfectly formed, so tiny, so early. Would there be a miracle? Would Connor survive the trauma of premature birth? He had a strong heartbeat, but his lungs were not fully developed. He was fighting to live. Every day was critical.

Every day, we were privileged to watch the baby's development, heretofore observed only by God in the womb. Each day, he grew. One week went by. At ten days the doctors thought life support should be turned off, but the kids said no. Two weeks, then three. Connor struggled against the tubes and tried hard to open his eyes. One day there was hope. The next, a setback.

At one month Connor was in crisis. Again, the doctors encouraged Heidi and Mel to take him off life support. The doctors felt Connor would have severe problems if he lived.

As Christians, we did not want to give up on God and prayed that He might do a miracle. But sometimes God does say no. Our prayer was that God would take him and the kids would not have to live with the decision to take him off the machines.

Heidi went shopping for burial clothes. She couldn't find anything small enough, so she asked me to look. In The Doll Shop, a caring clerk and I had almost given up when she remembered an outfit that was not on display. It had a nautical theme, and Connor's daddy likes sailboats. It was perfect. Made for a thirteen-inch doll, it was a little big but perfect nonetheless.

As I walked into the hospital room with the clothes, I was stunned to see Connor in the arms of his mother! It was the first time she had been allowed to hold him. Both parents were ecstatic.

At first I was fearful that the end was near and that was why the doctors had allowed this joyous event to take place. But no. Connor, still in crisis, had opened his eyes and was looking, unseeing I'm sure, at his mother, following the soft, gentle sound of her voice. We took pictures and rejoiced. It was an unforgettable moment to be repeated only one more time.

At seven weeks the baby weighed two pounds, fourteen ounces. There was still hope we might be allowed to keep this tiny one. Then on September 28, 1993, at three o'clock in the morning, another crisis, the last.

Once again, the doctors encouraged Heidi and Mel to shut down the machines. They could not. Just as the doctor turned to do that, Connor's heartbeat stopped. It was a real answer to prayer. We had prayed over and over to God, "You know what to do. Connor is in your hands, God, and we know you know what to do."

Gracious God honored our constant prayer and took Connor Himself, naturally. There would be no miracle this time.

The hardest thing about losing a grandbaby like this is watching the pain as your own children go through it and knowing there's nothing you can do but hold them and pray constantly.

Heidi and Mel have been greatly helped by a support group called P.S. The P.S. stands for "Parents of Stillbirth." The organization ministers to parents after miscarriage, stillbirth, and early infant death.

God taught us much through this time. Many wonderful people have loved us through this tragic loss. We are more sensitive and loving toward our kids now, more open with our emotions. We express our feelings by touching and hugging and have a new appreciation for the fragility and preciousness of life. We know that all things work together for good, and we talk about that candidly, always looking to the future and the blessings God has in store for all of us.

And God is blessing this family. They are stronger for having been broken. United in their Christian faith, they look forward with great anticipation and joy to a new birth! Heidi is expecting another child in October 1994.

SUDDEN INFANT DEATH SYNDROME

In the January 1985 Educational Ministries bulletin for the American Baptist Churches Association in which he served, Pastor Gay Hasselblad wrote of a prized Christmas gift received from his four-month-old grandson, Jordan. The new license plate holder read "Happiness is being a grandparent." Pastor Hasselblad proclaimed a new personal resolution. In addition to other identities as a Christian, husband, father, and servant in the church, he now joyously resolved be a godly grandparent.

In the very next month's bulletin Grandpa Hasselblad sorrowfully reported the grievous news of the death of his precious grandson, a victim of Sudden Infant Death Syndrome (SIDS). Beautiful, healthy, four-month-old Jordan died during a nap at the babysitter's, next door to the home of his parents, Rick and Cindi Hasselbad, on January 10, 1985.

But this tragedy was not to be the last in the Hasselblad grandparenting season. The family rejoiced at the birth of grandson Jacob on August 4, 1986, only to have to give him up as well on October 31 of that year to Sudden Infant Death Syndrome.

Two grandbabies lost to SIDS. Double SIDS deaths happen in approximately 7 in 100,000 births. How would the Hasselblad family cope? Here is the uplifting story from these loving Christian grandparents.

Grandpa Hasselblad: Both Jordan and Jacob enriched our lives. In the brief time we had with each of them, we recognized their special qualities and give thanks to God for sharing them with us. We do not understand why this happened. "Why" questions are for SIDS, not for God. We give them up reluctantly, knowing that they were each gifts of grace to us from our heavenly Father in whose presence they have taken a new form. Jordan and Jacob are with us still, in our thoughts and hearts, never to be forgotten.

Through this most difficult time, we are filled with gratitude for the members of the household of faith, our local church family, who have offered a caring ministry of healing and hope. Their loving, thoughtful nurturing has ministered to us in marvelous, meaningful ways. In the words of our dear pastor, Rodney Romney, at one of the services for our grandsons at First Baptist Church, Seattle: "Isaiah was gloriously right when he said, 'A little child shall lead them.'"

Our lives had been led and guided to a time to come together, to pray together, and seek God's comfort together. Neither Jordan nor Jacob had the chance to form their character or to do a full life's work. But they had the chance to be loved by parents who wanted them and who prayed for their coming and to bring great happiness to the hearts of their grandparents and to all who knew them. We know God has hold of Jordan and Jacob, just as He does each of us. And God will never let us go. The poet Kahlil Gibran said,

Your children are not your children.
They are the sons and daughters of Life's longing for itself.

They come through you but not from you,
And though they are with you, yet they belong not to you.

So we say goodbye to two of God's tiny children and, in doing so, we offer ourselves boldly, saying "God, our God, Thy will be done." We are to trust God, to love Him and cherish the knowledge that He loves us.

Grandma Hasselblad: God's grace to us has been evident throughout our lives, but never more apparent than as we lived through the devastating losses of our two grandsons. Our son, Rick, and his wife, Cindi, have been an inspiration by their courage and abiding faith in nearly unbearable moments. They sought counseling, and for years now, both have served on the board of the Sudden Infant Death Syndrome Foundation, helping others cope with their loss and promoting research to find the cause of SIDS.

God taught me that His grace is sufficient for one day and that I start all over the next day with a fresh supply. He graciously gave me a grief partner who helped me tremendously, and now I am able to help someone else. God's love has been showered upon us through the faith community of His people.

Twenty months after Jacob's death, on June 21, 1988, God blessed Cindi and Rick with the birth of twins, Nathan and Kelsey. All of us spent that anxious first year of their lives on our knees. Cindi had promised a huge celebration on the twins' first birthday. We had an unforgettable birthday party with many friends and family members who had been praying right along with us!

The SIDS Foundation hosts an annual celebration of the lives of SIDS babies at a local church. When the twins were three, Rick and Cindi took them to the event. At the close of the program of remembering, everyone went outside the building and was given a balloon to be released in memory of one who had died. Nathan's balloon slipped out of his hand before he was ready to let it go. He began to cry. His twin sister, Kelsey, comforted him, saying, "Oh, that's OK, Nathan. Jordan and Jacob will be able to play with it."

As many as seven thousand babies die of SIDS every year in America. This mysterious killer usually strikes when a baby is between the ages of two and four months, only rarely after twelve months. For some unknown reason, SIDS babies just stop breathing.

James J. McKenna, Ph.D., professor of anthropology at Pomona College in Claremont, California, is one of the leading

researchers currently focusing on SIDS. He offers the following good information for grandparents and others caring for
infants:

> "We don't know what causes SIDS. The most compel-
> ling general hypothesis about the primary cause of SIDS is
> that the fatal event occurs during sleep. As a result, the
> patterns of infant sleep, breathing, and arousal are being
> intensely studied. One study suggests a contributing factor
> might be lack of breastfeeding. Another is looking at the
> issue of too much bundling up in cold weather. According
> to several recent studies, infants who sleep face down may
> be at greater risk, especially those sleeping on cushions
> where they might be unable to dislodge themselves from
> pockets formed by the cushions."[4]

As we pray for the cause of this dreaded syndrome to be
discovered, we arm ourselves to deal with it, should it happen.
Grandma Hasselblad has this sage advice for grandparents
who experience a grandchild's death from SIDS:

1. Allow people to talk about it.
2. Have a service! It gives the whole family a time and place
   to grieve and say goodbye.
3. Accept people's expressions of love, even when the words
   don't come out quite right. The intent is there.
4. Do not hesitate to talk about the baby by name.
5. Support the parents and siblings.
6. Remember that as believers, we know that God's love is as
   strong through this crisis and as perfect as always. He does
   not allow crisis to test us but to show us His love and grace.

Grandchildren Living with HIV and AIDS

Treasua (pronounced "Tresh-a") is a healthy, chubby, playful,
strong-willed six-year-old who lives with her fifty-two-year-
old grandmother, Liz. Treasua's name is derived from the word

treasure, which is exactly what she is to her devoted grand-mother, who has raised her granddaughter from birth and has legal custody. Treasua's four-year-old brother, Hakim, lives in another state. He lived his first few months in an environment of poverty and violence with his mother, a crack cocaine addict. Hakim was placed in foster care with a couple that hopes to adopt him. Grandma Liz regrets that she hasn't seen her grandson in over two years.

Both Treasua and Hakim are HIV positive. Both innocent children will eventually develop AIDS. Neither has been told. Read what Liz has to say, and imagine what this brave grand-mother faces on a daily basis just to provide a sense of home and family for her granddaughter.

> It's not that I am in denial. Someday, I'll have to tell Treasua she's sick. Right now, she's not sick. I give her AZT medicine. She's heard about AIDS in school and has asked me questions. She may suspect something. For the last couple of years, she has tended to speak about herself as if she were someone else. Her prayers at night close with, "Dear God, bless Treasua. Help Treasua to be good and grow her up to be a teenager."

> I deal with her illness one day at a time. I just thank God every day and every night for putting Treasua in my life. I love her so much. I don't ask God 'why?' I have a strong faith in the Creator. All things are possible through Him. He's in charge. I am so thankful for the blessings in my life. We attend church, and the pastor and other Christian friends are praying for us. One day at a time. We'll be all right.

During 1992, state and territorial health departments in America reported 47,095 cases of acquired immunodeficiency syndrome (AIDS) to the Centers for Disease Control, an increase of 3.5 percent over 1991. The CDC reports that over half of these cases were attributable to homosexual/bisexual men, a fact at the root of one of the great church debates of all time involving the compassion of Christ and God's Word in Romans 1:24.

Projections indicate a steady increase in the number of AIDS cases—approximately 150,000 cases by 1995. In the latest figures, heterosexual contact accounted for the largest proportionate increase of reported cases, followed by an increase in the numbers of children with the disease. In 1989 and 1990, there were approximately six thousand babies born to HIV-infected women. Another one thousand are expected to be born *per year* during the period April 1990 through December 1994.

There is another harsh reality that is sometimes overovershadowed by the more obvious tragedies related to this deadly syndrome. More and more children are faced with losing their HIV positive parents. Humanitarian organizations are ministering to children whose parents (or themselves) have either HIV or AIDS.

Jan is a young, compassionate grandmother who volunteers at a camp for kids dealing with the disease. "A few weeks ago, I held Rebecca," Jan shared. "As we sat together in her tent, uncontrolled sobs shook her small body. 'Daddy's leaving. I don't want him to go. I hate AIDS. They buy me presents, but I don't want presents. I want them to stop fighting, and I want the AIDS to go away.'"

"Yesterday, I met Jessie. Her mother has AIDS. Jessie is not infected. We sat in her father's van chatting about dreams. Jessie hasn't been exposed to the violence of television and other societal ills. Jessie still talks to angels. Her dad and many other people will help her to stay her sweet, hopeful self."

We can all draw inspiration and hope from these and other Christian grandparents walking through the valleys of loss and from those who minister to them. Using the most powerful weapon God has given us by His grace, please pray for them and for their loved ones.

GRACE PRINCIPLE:

God's grace is real.

*But I do not account my life of any value nor as precious to
myself, if only I may accomplish my course
and the ministry which I received from the Lord Jesus,
to testify to the gospel of the grace of God*

— Acts 20:24, RSV

The next chapter examines the serious plight of millions
of grandparents faced with parenting all over again.

PART FIVE

WHEN THE "GRAND" IS GONE

*T*wo men were fishing in a river when an infant floated past. The first fisherman jumped in, rescued the child, and handed him up to safety in the second fisherman's arms. No sooner had they settled the child down on the grass, when a second infant floated along. Again, the fisherman jumped in and rescued the baby. A third baby floated along, a fourth, and so on. The fisherman saved each in turn. Finally, a whole group of babies came floating downstream. The first fisherman grabbed as many as he could and looked up to see his friend walking away. "Hey," he shouted, "what's wrong with you? Aren't you going to help me save these babies?" The second fisherman replied, "You save these babies. I'm going upstream to see who's throwing all these babies into the river."[1]

Today, millions of children are being "thrown into the river" and saved by their *grandparents*. For grandparents raising their own grandchildren, fighting for custody of a grandchild, or seeking visitation, grandparenting has changed and will never be the same again. For them, the "grand" is gone.

ॐ

Chapter 16

GRANDPARENTS RAISING GRANDCHILDREN

Tom and Mary Fron dreamed about what life would be like after the last of their four teenagers moved out. They would buy a cabin in the northern Michigan woods and spend weekends snowmobiling. Just the two of them.

Then sixteen-year-old Betsy, their youngest, announced she was pregnant. The Frons soon found they were not grandparents, but Mom and Dad. Again.

They adopted Nathan, now five, when their unmarried daughter proved too immature to care for him and moved out. The Frons shuffled their work schedules to avoid day-care costs. The money they had saved for a vacation cabin pays for Nathan's preschool.

"I wouldn't give him up for anything," Mrs. Fron said. "But there are wild days when he's playing his flute and has his dog romping with him in the house, and there is a smidgen of resentment that this isn't what I expected."

So much for baking cookies and occasional babysitting. Nowadays, being a grandparent can turn into a twenty-four-hour-a-day job.

The change in grandparenting over the last several decades is being graphically lived out by grandparents who have become the parent of their own grandchildren because of the choices and circumstances of their adult children's lives. Exhibiting courage that could only come from God, grandparents are becoming parents all over again.

The reasons for this sad phenomenon are:

- ❖ Substance abuse
- ❖ Divorce
- ❖ Physical, sexual, emotional abuse
- ❖ Teen pregnancy
- ❖ Abandonment
- ❖ Neglect
- ❖ Suicide
- ❖ AIDS
- ❖ Accidental death
- ❖ Imprisonment
- ❖ Mental Illness

The 1990 Census says that 3.3 million of American's children live in a home maintained by a grandparent, up one million from 1980. Of those, 937,000 children, or about 1.3 percent of our nation's youth, live with grandparents in homes where neither parent is present, as the chart on the following page shows.[1]

Black and Hispanic children, especially those living in cities struggling with crack cocaine and AIDS, are more likely to live in a home maintained by a grandparent. The Census Bureau found 12 percent of black children living in a grandparent's home, compared to 6 percent of Hispanic children and less than 4 percent of white children.

Nevertheless, about 60 percent of grandparents raising grandchildren are white. Many are affluent, according to Meredith Minkler, professor of public health at the University of California at Berkeley.

"Grandparent care cuts across class and ethnic group lines," Minkler said.[2]

Grandchildren (under 18) living with grandparents:

	1980	1991
	2,306,000	3,320,00 up 1 million
With both parents present	310,000	559,000
With only mother present	922,000	1,674,000
With only father present	86,000	151,000
With neither parent present	988,000	937,000

Tom and Mary Fron, forty-seven and forty-six, respectively, are among the young grandparents. However, most grandparents raising children again are beyond the typical childrearing age. Preliminary studies at Berkeley show more than half are fifty-five or older and one quarter are sixty-five or older. For the older ones, especially, serving as parents again takes a toll.

Childrearing grandparents range in age from the late twenties to the early nineties. I have attended grandparent support group meetings where grandparents who are obviously too old and infirm to handle the responsibility bring their small grandchildren, having no one to sit for them. They come seeking resources, legal help, and emotional support.

Several months ago, a twenty-eight-year-old grandmother approached me after a seminar to ask for prayer for her fourteen-year-old daughter who did just what her mother had done. A three-month-old baby girl, a mother, now fifteen, and a grandmother were trying, by God's grace, to make a new start. I will never forget that day. Several prayed for them, that the generational sin would stop with this beautiful new baby girl. I feel confident that God is blessing this trio with a loving church family and Christian role models for the future.

Situations of grandparents involved in raising their grandchildren vary widely. Some grandparents are legally in charge of their grandchildren through adoption, legal custody, or guardianship, as you will read in the next chapter. Still other grandparents take on parenting responsibilities informally, often with their child's approval and/or cooperation. These informal "caretakers" are hard to count. Experts say their numbers are also in the millions.

Grandparents most often take legal steps for two reasons:

1. The parents cannot or will not take responsibility for the child. Drug and alcohol dependence, emotional problems, and "still sowing wild oats" are common explanations.

2. Health insurers often require legal custody to put a grandchild on the grandparent's policy. Getting a single health
   insurance policy for the child is much more expensive.

The emotional toll for these new "parents" is extremely
high. John and his wife, Alice, supported their daughter, Ann,
when she moved back into their home with four-year-old
grandson, Bobby. They juggled their work and home schedules
to provide care for Bobby while Ann socialized. "We love
Bobby," Alice said, "but it would be best for everyone if Ann
found somebody else and remarried." "And moved out,"
added John.

Eileen, a widowed grandparent with health problems, got
a call from a social services agency. "We found your grandchild
alone in a playpen after a neighbor called about the crying. The
neighbor says it is not the first time, and we cannot locate your
son or his wife. Will you take the child? If not, she will be placed
in foster care while we determine what to do." Eileen agreed
and eventually went to court to get legal custody of her granddaughter. "I'd do anything before I would see that child go into
the system as it is today," Eileen said.

A young pastor's eighteen-year-old daughter, Laura, became pregnant and told her parents she wished to live with the
father of the child. She was a Baptist girl, raised in the home
of a Baptist preacher. The anguished grandparents-to-be were
not yet forty. They encouraged their daughter and prayed for
her and for the baby. By the time the baby had arrived, Laura
had changed her mind about moving out. Today, she is attending college while her parents provide daily care and nurture
for the child.

Stories like these are becoming commonplace in America.
In 1992, Dr. Margaret Platt Jendrek of Miami University sur-
veyed 114 Ohio grandparents. The results of that study and
others typify the profound adjustments made by sacrificing
grandparents.

- ❖ Missing the peace and privacy of the "empty nest."
- ❖ Changing routines to accommodate a three-year-old's needs.
- ❖ Using up their retirement savings.
- ❖ Giving up their retirement dreams.
- ❖ Longtime friends who don't come over any more.
- ❖ Up all night with an infant.
- ❖ Struggling with discipline problems.
- ❖ Fighting court battles, often against their own child.
- ❖ Rifts with other family members over their parenting role.
- ❖ Long marriage strained to the breaking point with grand-children in the house.[3]

A BRIEF PROFILE

Who are these saints tackling parenthood all over again? They are people like you and me. Their ages range from twenty-eight to the nineties. Most of them are white. Some feel alone and isolated, knowing no one else in their situation. Some lack the support of a helpful family or may have few, if any, friends who understand their new situation. Some have to stop work to raise their grandchildren. They are all dealing with heavy emotional, relational issues, while finding it difficult, at best, to have their own needs met or to continue the activities they once enjoyed.

Most grandparents raising their own grandchildren admit to kaleidoscopic feelings of anger, grief, and self-pity. They see that they cannot make up for what the children have not had in the past but can work on the here and now of building a foundation of trust, love, and security.

Some are targets of their grandchildren's anger and, at times, rage they feel toward their parents and others. Grand-father is the more authoritarian figure in the home. Grand-mother is more easily manipulated, especially by teenage grandchildren. Frequently, grandmother and grandfather have conflicting ideas about the way the children should be dealt with. This may result in grandmother overcompensating for the stern attitude of her husband. Resentment develops in long-standing marriages.

Grandparents complain of being "robbed" of the traditional role of "doting" grandparent. Grandparents with health problems, such as poor vision and arthritis, find their own health care coming in second to meeting the needs of grandchildren. Counselors say poverty fuels the fire, as some grandmothers will pay up to $100 for brand name sneakers for a grandchild, while they wear $4 shoes themselves.

In addition to the stresses of parenting, grandparents raising grandchildren often have expensive court battles going on for the best interest of the child. They endure with one overriding emotion—love for their grandchildren.

WHO ARE THESE GRANDCHILDREN?

Grandchildren being raised by their grandparents look very much like your grandchildren and mine. They are mostly white but come from every socioeconomic level, race, color, and creed. They are children caught between warring parents, or parents and grandparents, or grandparents and the system. Or they are children caught in a web of poverty, abuse, and neglect. For many, hopes and dreams have been dashed and now, the most important persons in their lives are their grandparents, their thread to reality and to the future.

They are children like eleven-year-old Monique, who said, "I just don't know why my Mom does what she does. I know she loves me. She told me so. But she does bad things, and she takes drugs. Why can't she just stop and be my Mom? I love my Grandma, but my Mom is my Mom. I miss her so much!"

SUPPORT GROUPS

In the half light of the big room, a grandmother in the last row of chairs stood to ask if anyone else had a daughter in prison. A little later a grandfather pleaded for a source of financial relief as sole support for three teenage grandsons. Sitting next to him, a grandmother of thirty-six cradled an infant grandbaby in her arms as she glanced nervously at the doorway to see if she had been followed to the meeting by the baby's father.

To help grandparents like these, more than 350 grandparent support groups have sprung up all over America in the last two years, and the list is growing. Groups meet in churches, clinics, schools, doctors' offices, or counselors' homes.

Dedicated social workers conduct some of these meetings on their own time because they see the great need in their daily work. Others are led by a compassionate, knowledgeable grandparent who is experienced in this sacrificial work and who wants to pass expertise and resources on to others. All would like very much to work themselves out of a job.

Some support groups have newsletters alerting members to new legislation or needed resources, encouragement, and success stories. Most grandparent support groups are grass roots organizations running on a financial shoestring of meager donated funds.

Grandparents Raising Grandchildren, Inc. is a three-state consortium of support groups in Washington, Oregon, and Idaho, whose stated mission is: "To make the world a safer place for those children whose birth parents are unable or unwilling to assume the legal and moral responsibilities of parenthood; unable or unwilling to provide the safety, stability and nurturing guaranteed the children of these states; and to educate ourselves on the legal aspects of custody, visitation and adoption and the legal rights of all parties."[4]

Another group lists their goals as:

- ❖ To help reduce stress felt by grandparents raising grandchildren.
- ❖ To develop a support network between these grandparents.
- ❖ To provide the opportunity to verbalize and share feelings and unique issues grandparents as parents face in a warm, supportive environment. Topics include anger toward their children for shirking parental responsibility, resentment toward grandchildren, feelings of missing out on being grandparents, and positive feelings and experiences of grandparenting.

Agendas for grandparent support group meetings vary but are generally flexible, allowing everyone in the room to talk about their situation. Some are reluctant to speak up, but not for long. Those who are experiencing similar problems eventually cluster to share together. Grandparents who attend for the first time express, often tearfully, relief at being able to tell someone else about the circumstances surrounding their grandchild(ren).

Often a special speaker is invited: a judge, a family law attorney, a child advocate, or a social worker to talk about a specific issue facing grandparents as parents, how to work with the system and not against it, or to take questions from the group. Those who accept these invitations are brave to come, because they can be verbally pummeled by emotional grandparents who feel that the system is insensitive to their needs and to the needs of their grandchild(ren).

- ❖ "I tried that in my county, and it didn't work!"
- ❖ "Why can't I be allowed to speak up in court? I've been taking care of this child for years, and I don't even have a chance to be heard on his behalf!"
- ❖ "You can't tell me you have my grandchild's 'best interests' at heart! We've been shuffled from one person to the next and still don't have any answers!"

It is good to see that there are those in positions of authority who will come to experience firsthand the frustrations,
anger, and soul-deep sorrow of grandparents who stand in as
parents. No doubt these speakers leave with a new appreciation
for grandparents who raise their own grandchildren.

Mostly, grandparent support groups are a safe place to talk
with people going through similar circumstances and to be
pointed in the right direction for help desperately needed.

What Are the Needs?

The needs of grandparents raising grandchildren are many
and varied.

Financial Assistance

The only monetary help for a grandparent raising a grandchild comes from Aid for Dependent Children, which varies
from state to state and is never enough. It can also appear
inequitable. For example, in one state, AFDC pays $349 for one
child, $440 for two. "Interesting," commented one grandpar-
ent, "that one child is worth less than another."

Grandparents raising grandchildren apply for AFDC
funds by filling out a form at their local Department of Social
& Health Services office. If a grandparent raising a grandchild
is retired, that grandparent may apply for Social Security
benefits if the child is formally adopted by the grandparent.
For information on Social Security or supplemental Social
Security benefits, contact the reference department of your
local library or your Social Security office.

One of the kindest, most helpful things one can do for a
grandparent raising a grandchild is to pay their legal fees.
Those of us blessed with more of the Lord's money than
another might prayerfully consider this kind of support. Most
grandparents raising grandchildren are on a limited income.
Their only motivation is the best interest of their grandchild.

Emotional Support

Grandparents complain of lack of support from family members. David and June Barry are an example. Their son became a father while in the service. The mother, an alcoholic, has primary custody of the child. The son and his parents are fighting an intensive legal battle for the well-being of the child, whose mother is neglectful to the point of abandonment. As the grandparents and the son fear for the very life of the boy, family members remain distant, even critical of their efforts.

Reparenting Classes

Grandparents who take the role of parent today are finding their grandchildren growing up in a very different world than that of their birth children. What do you feed a child today? How do you discipline a child today? How do you fold a diaper?

Our children didn't have to deal with drive-by shootings, gangs, drugs, and weapons in school. Personal safety at home, on school grounds, and in the streets is on the minds of every parent today. It is, therefore, also constantly on the mind of grandparents raising their grandchildren. Video games; sex and violence on television and in movies; the unrealistic expectations created by the media for America's children to be thin, rich, and famous; and the rock stars, models, overpaid athletes, and other '90s role models all portray a sinful world.

Grandparents raising grandchildren need free classes that will arm them with the same survival techniques that young parents learn. Hospital staff, community colleges, and social service agencies are recognizing the need and offering real support in these areas.

Community Support

In addition to reparenting classes, grandparents raising grandchildren need social service agencies and community-based resources to step in with respite care, discipline training, and counseling for the children from abusive backgrounds. If you or someone you know needs help, contact any local senior assistance group in your area. Senior assistance groups have different names such as Seniors Rights or Counsel on Aging, but in every county there is an office on aging for seniors. Many have new, innovative programs for grandparents.

Discipline can be an especially difficult problem for grandparents raising grandchildren, because often, they are dealing with children that have suffered physical or emotional damage. Kids with Attention Deficit Disorder (ADD), for example, or kids with abuse symptoms must be treated individually. Public education support is also being encouraged to bring the necessary resources to these grandparents.

Support for New Legislation

Because of extensive federal government land holdings, America has a federal law protecting its animals. America has no federal law to protect its children. The "best interests" of a child is currently a state-by-state issue, and some states are recognizing the critical role played by grandparents who are raising their own grandchildren as well as the unprecedented needs of children in general.

We can all be encouraged by that, and support lawmakers' efforts by watching for new legislation to assist grandparents in their needs as outlined above and writing and/or telephoning our support to state and county officials.

Prayer

Grandparents who are parenting grandchildren need prayer. Those saints who know the Lord need prayer. And those who have not yet accepted the only One who can give them that peace of spirit that passes all understanding need prayer. If it were possible to count the numbers, probably over seven million grandparents are doing this miracle work, almost all of them at great personal sacrifice to the hopes and dreams they had for their later years. Will you commit to pray for just one of them? We know from Scripture and from God's grace in our own lives that the power of righteous prayer availeth much.

A New National Resource

In September 1993, the American Association of Retired Persons (AARP) established an information clearinghouse to help the growing number of grandparents raising grandchildren. The Center in Washington, D.C., was established with a three-year, $300,000 grant from the Brookdale Foundation Group, a philanthropic organization in New York, to work with grandparent support groups and other national and community-based groups, as well as agencies dealing with aging, child care, legal services, and family services.

Until a toll-free line is installed, long distance callers to the AARP Grandparent Information Center may call 1-202-434-2296, leave their number, and have their calls returned. Information available through the center includes the nearest support group in your area, help with questions about custody, health insurance, welfare benefits, and other issues of importance to grandparents raising grandchildren.

The Positives of Parenting Again

Not all grandparents raising grandchildren are unhappy in their situations. Tina and George received their grandson Michael, when he was three.

> Our daughter, Samantha, never bonded with her son. We watched our grandson living without maternal love and affection and got ahold of him every chance we could get. Finally, when Samantha had gone through several drug rehabilitations, only to go back to her same abuse habits and live-in situations, we took Michael for good. We legally adopted him last year. We are thrilled to have him. We are

in our late sixties, but having Michael brings such joy to our lives. He's a good boy, smart as a whip. At six, he's in school now and doing just fine. We feel very blessed to have him in our home and will give him the best possible future.

Another grandmother gets great enjoyment from seeing her husband have the time and inclination to relate to his grandson in a way he never had with his children. Other grandparents have developed a special relationship with their grandchildren and are quite relaxed about being parents again, some saying they are not as strict or anxious as they were with their own children.

But the majority of parenting grandparents are beleaguered. They thought this season of their life would be filled with relaxation and the joys of being a real grandparent. The following salutes, written by anonymous grandchildren, describe the heart of millions of grandparents in America today who are parenting all over again:

A Mom

She talks like a Mom. She acts like a Mom.
She looks like a Mom. She was there when
I said my first words. She was there on my
first day at kindergarten. She took care of
me when I fell off my bicycle. She wiped away
my tears when Grandpa died. She attended my
first piano recital and when I made the goal
for my soccer team and when I struck out at bat.
She came and got me from the vice-principal's
office when I got in trouble. She's there when
I come home from school. She loves like a Mom.
She's my Grandma.

Grandfathers Are to Love

Sometime between when you put away your blocks
and tomorrow when you put on your sox,

someone will be thinking of you. He is grandfather.
Grandfathers come in all sizes,
tall or short, hairy or bald, thin and not-so-thin.
But more than that, they come when you need them.
They even let you call them Daddy when you need them.
Your big hugs and little kisses
are what grandfathers are made of.
Trusting and kind, grandfathers are to love.[5]

GRACE PRINCIPLE:

God's grace is sufficient.

"My grace is sufficient for you, for my power is made perfect in weakness."

— 2 Corinthians12:9, RSV

Next, we learn about grandparents who are faced with obtaining legal custody of a grandchild and the prospect of parenting again indefinitely.

ॐ

Chapter 17

GRANDPARENTS SEEKING CUSTODY

A grandparent support group leader told about the turmoil in the home of Sharon and Mark, who live on a farm and have had custody of their grandson from age two to twelve.

Their daughter has a long history of drug convictions. The father has never paid child support and has visited his son only twice in ten years. Without warning, the father petitioned the court to give custody of his son to him.

Authorities told Sharon and Mark that they have no voice in the matter and that the "best interests" of the child is served when one or both of the biological parents have custody. Their grandson does not want to leave the only home he knows to live with his father. The court will decide his future shortly.

Heart-wrenching stories like this one are common. Every state has laws governing custody. They vary from state to state, however. Thankfully, although far too slowly, laws are changing to include loving grandparents .

NONPARENTAL CUSTODY ACT

Washington is one of the few states which has a Parenting Act resolving custody issues by means of a nonadversarial Parent-

ing Plan instead of the traditional custody terminology. R.C.W.
(Revised Code of Washington) 26.10 allows grandparents to
petition the court for custody by proving that either (1) both
parents were unsuitable, or (2) that the child was not in the
custody of either parent.

This law for parents resulted in a separate law being passed
for third-party custody cases; in most cases, the "third party"
will be a grandparent or a stepparent who seeks custody of a
nonbiological child. Third party custody can also occur as the
fallout from a divorce between the parents, in which case the
grandparent would intervene as a party in the divorce action.

In order to be awarded custody, a grandparent is not
required to prove that the parents are unfit in the same sense
that the state must prove a parent unfit to remove a child from
that parent's home. Nevertheless, a grandparent must prove
that leaving the child with the parent would be detrimental to
the child's welfare.

Grandparents must always give both parents notice of
their intention to seek custody or guardianship, even if it
means publishing in the newspaper.[1]

GUARDIANSHIP AND CUSTODY

Many grandparents who have legal care of their grandchild
actually did not obtain the child by filing either a "custody" or
"guardianship" case. Often the Child Protective Service (having varying names in each state) has already removed the child
from one or both of the natural parents; their policy is to then
place the child (if possible) with a close family relative, usually
a grandparent.

The state Department of Social and Health Services maintains ultimate control of the child's placement. They can uni-
laterally remove the child from the grandparents and even
place the child in foster care if they feel this would be best. This
can and does happen where a state has instructed the grand-

parents to allow no contact (or supervised contact only) between child and parent and where a grandparent does not comply. If the child remains with the grandparent for a long period of time under state placement, eventually the state may encourage the grandparents to seek legal custody of the child on their own so that the state can withdraw from overseeing the child's placement.[2]

LOCATING, INTERVIEWING, AND HIRING AN ATTORNEY

Grandparents raising grandchildren need the advice of a competent attorney. For many grandparents, this is foreign territory. Where do you find a good attorney?

When looking for an attorney, a grandparent should insist upon someone (1) whose practice emphasizes family law; and (2) who has experience representing grandparents in third-party issues.

Do not look to attorney advertising to hire an attorney. Ask for personal referrals within a support group or contact a lawyer referral service in your community. They are listed in the phone book or your local library as "Attorney Referral Services" or "Lawyer Referral & Information Services." Or call your state Bar Association for assistance under the category of "grandparents rights."

It is also important for you to feel comfortable with your attorney. Is the attorney concerned about and attentive to your problems? Does he or she believe in your case? Will he or she be able to work through problems and disagreements with you and not just with the other side? Does he or she seem capable of effectively advocating for your position?

The attorney is your employee. You are entitled to ask questions regarding background, experience, and continuing education. This is important because some attorneys are reluctant to work with some agencies such as Child Protective Services and others. You need to know that.

Most attorneys will want an advance retainer before taking the case. In giving an attorney a retainer, you are merely prepaying for so many hours of his or her time, depending upon his or her hourly rate. If your case settles early or if for any reason you should drop the case, find out whether (and how much of) your retainer is refundable.

Hourly rates of attorneys vary according to experience. You will pay more for an experienced attorney, but often that attorney can accomplish more work in a shorter amount of time. *There is no substitute for experience.*

Ask if there is a qualified attorney in the firm who works *pro bono* (without charge). Some attorneys donate some of their time for the public good.

If you are working with a son or daughter's attorney regarding custody or visitation of a grandchild, you should retain an attorney of your own, separate from theirs.

Getting Educated

Custody battles require that participants know what they are dealing with going in. Grandparents would do well to familiarize themselves with terms they have heard but do not understand. Some examples follow.

Custody . . .

A legal proceeding in which the care, custody, and control of a child is given to someone other than the birth parents by order of the court. Custody can be permanent (until the child reaches majority) or temporary (for a specific length of time).

Adoption . . .

A proceeding in which the birth parents consent to have their parental rights terminated by the court. In some cases, such as incarceration of a parent (usually the mother but sometimes the father), the court may arbitrarily terminate the parental rights.

Open Adoption . . .

The parents consent to terminate their custody rights but retain visitation rights so the parent/child relationship is not completely severed. The adopting person will determine the visitation schedule. The advantage is that the adoptive parents have complete control of the child's life. Having the right of visitation and the elimination of financial support will soften the effect of the court's decision (and often the heart of an offending parent to the best interests of their child).

Mediation . . .

A method of settling disputes outside a court setting wherein parties to an action come together to reconcile differences through negotiation. (This is the Christian way, of course. When emotions run high, as they will, negotiation can only be accomplished through a skilled professional, a completely unbiased mediator.)

Restraining Order or No Contact Order

These may be granted by a judge to prevent a person from personal, written, or telephone contact, or to prevent a threatened act while a court case is being decided. There must be an action filed with the court before such an order can be requested (divorce, custody, adoption, etc.). At the conclusion of the action, the order can be made permanent.

Guardian Ad Litem . . .

A person appointed by the court to oversee the welfare of a child in legal disputes. This person may be an attorney or a layperson but is expected to act impartially in submitting reports to the court. If at any time the conduct of the Guardian *Ad Litem* seems improper, the grandparent or other person directly involved with the case may file a complaint with the court. (A case in point would be the guardian who is a close friend of the opposing attorney or the caseworker.)

Psychological Evaluators

The court may order a psychological evaluation of both parties seeking custody. Are they mentally healthy? How do they relate to the child and the child to them? What kind of homes do they have? How do they do in psychological testing? Are they addicted to drugs or alcohol? Certainly an evaluation by a psychologist or psychiatrist can be helpful to the court.

Christians want to trust others to do the right thing. One embattled grandfather quoted an old Arabic saying, "Trust the Lord but tie your camel." Know what you're up against.

A MOTIVATION CHECK

Legal custody to protect you and your grandchild can be very expensive. One couple fought three years, spending more than $100,000 to gain custody of a grandson, and lost.

Legal custody is an explosive, many-sided issue. Emotions play a large role in the outcome. Sometimes grandparents have their own agenda, and what they want for a grandchild is not actually what is in the child's best interests.

In one case a daughter did indeed get her life straightened out. When she tried to retrieve her child, Grandma refused to give the child up. An emotional, costly legal battle ensued, mother against daughter. Grandma lost. Can you imagine going to court against a daughter or a son? It is bad enough when it is the only alternative for serving the best interests of a child. It is unconscionable when it is not necessary.

Putting first what is right and good for the child's future is not only the way legal authorities will evaluate the issue of custody, but it is always the most loving approach for a grandparent who wishes to have continued impact in a child's life.

A JUDGE SPEAKS THE TRUTH

Love is the motivator for grandparents wanting the best for grandchildren. Following a custody battle in the Superior

Court of the state of South Carolina in 1993, Judge A.J. Toal commented on the importance of love in a child's life:

> Only a child who has at least one person whom he can love, and who also feels loved, valued and wanted by that person, will develop a healthy self-esteem. He can then become confident of his own chances of achievement in life and convinced of his own human value. Where this positive environmental attitude toward an infant is missing from the start, the consequences become obvious in later childhood and adult life. They take the form of the individual's diminished care for the well-being of his own body, or for his physical appearance and clothing, or for his image presented to his fellow beings. What is damaged is his love and regard for himself, and consequently his capacity to love and care for others including his own children.[3]

Judge Toal describes the current state of affairs for millions of children caught in the middle of custody battles. Today we see the fruits of years of neglect in these children who have grown to adulthood. It must change—our future is at stake.

GRACE PRINCIPLE:

God's grace is free.

The Spirit and the bride say, "Come!" . . . Whoever is thirsty, let him come; and whoever wishes, let him take the free gift of the water of life.

— Revelation 22:17

In chapter 18, we look at grandparents who have been deprived of being with their beloved grandchildren due to disagreement with the parents or other circumstances.

℮

GRANDPARENTS SEEKING VISITATION

Like custody disagreements, visitation battles can prove to be so detrimental to the child in question that the process and the aftermath deeply wound the child, leaving scars that last for a lifetime.

Think about this. If a child really likes two friends who don't like each other and sees one friend on one side of the cafeteria and the other on the opposite side of the cafeteria, what agony of decision does the child face when he or she decides where to sit? Multiply that agony a thousand times, and that is what children feel when their parents, grandparents, and other adults in their lives whom they love are perceived by the child not to like each other. The agony is intensified when the child sees himself or herself as the "prize" to be won or lost in legal disputes.

This sobering scenario was described by Richard S. Victor, founder and executive director of Grandparents Rights Organization (GRO), headquartered in Birmingham, Michigan, in his acclaimed GRO National Newsletter. Attorney Victor represented the interests of "Baby Jessica" in the famous De-Boer visitation and custody trial and is well known for his work on behalf of grandparents and grandchildren throughout the

United States. In 1993, the National Council of Juvenile and Family Court Judges presented Mr. Victor their highest award for "Meritorious Service to the Children of America."

A grandparent's right to visit grandchildren would seem undeniable. Yet disputes arise between family members that cause agony and deep cracks in relationships with minor grandchildren.

THIRD PARTY RIGHTS TO VISITATION

Attorney Victor says that, as with custody, all fifty states have laws addressing the issue of grandparent visitation. In many states, legislatures enacted laws providing rights for grandparent visitation only following the death of a parent, leaving a minor child surviving. In those cases, grandparents (usually the parent of the deceased parent) would have a right to request and secure visitation with a surviving grandchild if the surviving parent denied access to the child.

When the surviving parent remarries and allows the new stepparent to adopt the child, many states have authorized an exception to the adoption codes to allow access or visitation by a biological grandparent even though the subsequent stepparent adoption would otherwise terminate the bloodline running from the deceased parent. Some states require a grandparent to file a request for visitation prior to the stepparent adoption. If they do not, they run the risk of being barred once the stepparent adoption has been finalized.

In other types of adoption cases where other than a stepparent is adopting the child, the termination of a parent's rights and subsequent adoption of the child would terminate any rights of the grandparent within that same bloodline to request visitation with the child. A grandparent who is denied contact with a grandchild should do the following:

1. Attempt to diffuse problems between their own family members before consulting an attorney to file a legal ac-

tion. This can be accomplished by telephone, written communication, or through face-to-face meetings.

2. In face-to-face meetings, avoid confrontational and accusatory statements. Remember that you all have one thing in common, the best interests of the child. A neutral behavioral science specialist is suggested as moderator.

3. Try again and again to resolve the dispute by coming to a reasonable, workable solution that reunites the entire family.

4. If family meetings fail or are denied, then litigation is an alternative.

5. In any attempt, avoid putting the child in the middle of emotional conflict between adults they love and respect but who do not show love and respect to one another.[1]

AFTER DIVORCE

Since most disputes arise following divorce, the custodial parent is the focus of the grandparent wishing to stay in touch with a grandchild. Studies have shown that multigenerational contact between children and their grandparents, and even great-grandparents, provides a special unconditional love and nurturing which is healthy for children. If death takes a grandparent from a grandchild, that is a tragedy. But if family bickering and vindictiveness deny a child the love of a grandparent, that is a shame.

If a divorce action has been filed by the parents, under most state laws, a grandparent would file a request for visitation in the county and before the judge who granted the divorce. This is done by a petition to intervene and a request for grandparent visitation in accordance with that state's specific statute, and they will vary from state to state.

If no divorce action was filed and a grandparent requests visitation following the death of a parent, then the action will be filed in the state and county where the child resides.

DEFINING "BEST INTERESTS"

Various factors are used in state statutes to define the "best interests" of the child in a visitation dispute.

1. Love, affection, and other emotional ties between the child and the grandparent.
2. The ability and disposition of the grandparent to provide the child with proper care while the child is in possession for visitation.
3. The prior relationship between the grandparent and the grandchild, including the history of contact or non-contact prior to the filing of the petition.
4. The moral fitness of the requesting grandparent.
5. The mental and physical health of the requesting grandparent.
6. The reasonable preference of the child if the court deems the child to be of a sufficient age to express a preference. (This is a particularly thorny issue according to grandparents whose older grandchildren are not given the right to speak for themselves in these matters.)
7. History of domestic violence involving the grandparent.

TERMS OF VISITATION

The extent and duration of visitation between a grandparent and a grandchild depend upon factors such as:

1. The age and health of the child.
2. Whether there is a visiting noncustodial parent and if so, the type of visitation schedule he/she exercises.
3. The geographic distance between the grandparent and grandchild.
4. The health and capacity of the grandparent to provide necessities for the grandchild while the child is with him or her.
5. The school and extracurricular schedule of the child.

VISITATION OF GRANDCHILDREN BORN OUT OF WEDLOCK

Limited rights presently exist for children born out of wedlock and their grandparents. Many states are now amending their laws to include children born out of wedlock in order to provide the children and grandparents equal protection. These actions are to be filed in the state and county where the parent raising the child resides.[2]

KEEPING GRANDPARENTS AWAY

In a recent survey for GRO, Marilyn Daniels discovered the not-so-surprising fact that former daughters-in-law make up the majority of parents involved in disputes over access to their children. She also reported some of the ways parents go about keeping the children away from their grandparents when they wish to close to door on past history.

1. Making visiting difficult or embarrassing.
2. Discouraging contact without actually forbidding it.
3. Creating deliberate "misunderstandings" about timing of visits, leaving grandparents waiting in their cars or on porches at an appointed visitation time.
4. Exerting negative pressure on the children, making them feel strange about being friendly toward their grandparents, and then using those awkward feelings expressed by the children as evidence that the children "didn't really like" or "didn't really know" the grandparents.
5. Making accusations of abuse or neglect against the grandparents. (Sadly, such accusations are sometimes true.)

KEEPING THE LINK

I never cease to be amazed at the creativity of grandparents! In the last several years, many of you have blessed me greatly as living examples of what I teach from the Word and know to be true, that...

Even when it appears hopeless, that you may never see a grandchild again in this life...

Even when a parent blocks your joy of being with a grandchild you love and miss so much...

Even then, you can accomplish your good and honorable purposes for that child. Let me share some great ideas you have given me.

A Quilt of Grandparent Love

Try to persuade the estranged parent to send you one piece of the child's clothing once a year in January, a shirt, a dress, a worn out coat. If the parent won't cooperate, then get it from a neighbor or other relative. Cut a square of cloth from that item and secretly sew it as one square in a "Quilt of Grandparent Love." On each square, embroider the year and one Scripture reference you prayed for the child that entire year that you did not see him or her. If you have items of clothing worn by the child in previous years, use them to make up for squares that might be missing.

Continue working faithfully on the quilt until your grandchild is of age. Then mail it to the child. If the child is barred from receiving mail from you, place the quilt in a bank vault or other place of safekeeping to be delivered to the child on the event of your death.

A grandchild who receives such a gift of ongoing love and dedication will know the truth of your love, no matter what the child has been told. Grandchildren grow up and discover who in the family told the truth and who really loves them.

Journaling a Testimony of Love

Journal the truth. Write in a journal—daily, weekly, or monthly, a "Testimony of Love" to the grandchild you no longer see. Write family history, stories about medical emergencies experienced when their father or mother was a child (this may be the child's only medical history link for the future).

Detail in your journal the day the child was born. Record your feelings about that day, what you remember of what their father said, how their mother looked. With everything you write, honor both parents as if no hard feelings had ever taken place. Remember the good times for your grandchild, never the bad. Most importantly, journal your faith in God for your grandchild to read.

Write about what times were like when you and your spouse were children, where you grew up, how you met, and what has happened to you since. Write about the happy times with their parent as that parent was growing up, and the funny things that happened. Write about holidays and birthdays. Thread the journal with exclamations of your love. Do not write about the painful fact of their absence in your life. They will know that.

If, as with the quilt, the journal cannot be mailed, place the journal in a bank vault or other safe place, marked, "To be delivered to _____ on the event of my death." It will be delivered. And the child will know.

Plan a Party

If birthday, Christmas, or other presents that you mail to your grandchild are returned to you marked "Unopened. Return to Sender," save them. Every one of them. Keep sending, receiving back, and saving. Put them in a closet.

It was a wise grandmother who gave me this idea. Though longing for a joy yet to be experienced, she said through her tears, "Some day that girl will be grown up. I am going to go get her, and we'll have a party to end all parties!"

God never gives us a difficult circumstance in life that He doesn't give us a way out. Hallelujah!

GRACE PRINCIPLE:

God precisely fits His grace to the need of the recipient.

"Before I formed you in the womb I knew you,
before you were born I set you apart."
— Jeremiah 1:5

As we leave this disturbing section of *Grandparenting by Grace,* we are reminded, as Jeremiah said, that God knows. Remember the joyful cry of Grandma Gloria in chapter 13?

You know, God! You know what is best. We trust You.
Thank You for Your love and grace to our family!

Let those comforting words be our leveler now as we learn how to model them for the generations and reflect upon the blessings of our lives.

ॐ

LOOKING TO THE TWENTY-FIRST CENTURY

I am a child of God.

  I have lived long.

  I have sinned and am forgiven.

  I have known joy.

  I have gained and am content.

  I have lost and am consoled.

  Underneath are the everlasting arms of Jesus.

  Deeper and deeper, the Holy Spirit indwells my soul.

  Dear one,

  All that I am, all that I possess

  Is but a whisper, a temporary legacy of things.

  The eternal legacy is not mine to give,

  Only mine to pass on.

  Above the clanging cymbals of the world,

  Listen for the still, small voice of God, saying,

  "Child of mine, I love you."

ॐ

Chapter 19

MODELING FOR THE GENERATIONS

As a nation, it is clear we haven't done a very good job of modeling for our children in the last several decades. Looking toward the twenty-first century, let us vow to make a difference for the generations to come, an individual difference! Throughout history, grandparents have stood for the faith as examples to others.

Ruthanne is a successful lawyer in a small town. She credits her grandfather for her diligent study habits; her ability to separate feelings from facts; and always remembering to pack honesty, integrity, and a Bible into her briefcase. She says, "By the way he lived his life and who he was in Christ, my grandfather was an example to me of what it really means to be a Christian."

God the Father intended that the character of Christ be His pattern for all generations to see, understand, feel, and model for others. Striving to emulate the true Christian character is an ongoing process, never completed. Keeping our eyes on Jesus, the perfect Model, His people are constantly learning how to honor God by allowing the Holy Spirit to produce His fruit in us (Gal. 5:22–25). Our loving God sends others into our lives who exhibit Christian character to us as we learn. In

Ruthanne's life, it was a grandparent who made a life-changing difference. So it was for Greg McNeece.

On the board of the South Carolina Southern Baptist Convention, Greg serves senior adults, singles, and families. One of the national leaders in Baptist senior adult ministry, some have asked how it is that one so young is so committed to senior adults. Here is Greg's moving testimony.

> My childhood was full of turmoil. My biological father decided he no longer wanted to be a father or a husband when I was one and one-half years old. My mother looked to her parents, my grandparents, as a source of support for both of us. Being a single mother raising a child in a small town in west Texas was unacceptable in 1970. My mom remarried when I was three. My stepfather did not like me. I remember fearing for my safety. During this entire marriage, my grandparents were my refuge. They extended to me love and security, something I never knew with my stepfather. The marriage lasted only a couple of years but yielded for me one of the great gifts of my life, my sister.
>
> My happiest childhood memories are of my grandparents, Paul and Dora Tibbets. They raised five children in a home that placed reverence upon the things of the Lord. Theirs was a home filled with love, joy, and happiness. I felt safe there.
>
> My grandparents were active members not only in the local Baptist Church of Anton, Texas, but they both held regional offices for the RSVP (Retired Senior Volunteer Program). I was one of the youngest persons ever to be a part of the RSVP at the ripe old age of four. I recall a crucial vote on something at a regional meeting. Both of my grandparents were opposed to the proposition and said they would resign if it was voted in. I popped off with, "And me, too!" which delighted my grandparents, I am told, and made a difference in the vote.

If Granny or Grandpa needed to put the fear of God into me, they relied on the local sheriff, whose name was Boots. I was terrified of Boots, so when I did anything wrong, my grandparents said they were going to tell Boots and, believe me, that kept me in line. One day, at the age of six, I tried to drive my Grandpa's car into the carport. I was just trying to be helpful. I got it started and as the car began to move forward, Grandpa jumped in and stopped it before it collided with the house. I remember a spanking that followed that occasion. Not only did the spanking reinforce my wrongdoing, but Grandpa said he would have to call Boots and tell him I was driving without a license. I was more afraid of that than I was the spanking. Needless to say, I had no desire to drive Grandpa's car, even just into the carport, until I was a licensed driver.

In my preteen years, I remember such happiness helping Granny and Grandpa push-plow the garden. I felt like I had an important part in making Granny's flowers grow and picking off the leaves from dying plants. Every day, my Grandpa would join several men at 9:15 A.M. at the local automotive store there in Anton. They would discuss the happenings of the day, what the weather was going to do, and what happened at church and at the senior citizen's center. I would pull up a stool alongside those men fifty or sixty years my senior and take part in their conversations. I loved it so very, very much, just being a part of their lives on a daily basis.

My grandparents instilled in me a love for service to the church. When I was twelve, my grandfather gave me a Bible that I still use today. When I open it, I think back to the fond memories my grandparents gave me. The time I watered the garden so much I sank into the soil up to my knees and Grandpa saved me. When Granny wanted to can bread and butter pickles and Grandpa and I went out to the onion processing plan southwest of Anton where they would give us as many onions as we wanted. I remember how my eyes watered and I'd have to go sit in the car. Grandpa and I loved to go fishing and camping, and I still do today.

So many memories. What my grandparents did for me was not only provide a place of safety and love, but they helped me understand the love of Jesus and His Lordship in our lives for *all* of our lives. My grandparents' love led me into a commitment of ministry to senior adults.

Greg's grandparents modeled their lives after the perfect model, Jesus. The major teachings and events of Jesus' brief life on earth gave us everything we need to do the same:

- ❖ The Commandments (Matt. 5:17–20; 22:36–40; John 13:34–35)
- ❖ *The Beatitudes* (Matt. 5:1–12)
- ❖ *The Great Commission* (Matt. 28:18–20; Acts 1:8)
- ❖ *Intercession* (Matt. 5:44; John 17)
- ❖ *His Life* (Luke 4:16–21; Acts 10:37,38)
- ❖ *His Death* (Isa. 53; Matt. 27:32–54; John 10:17–18)
- ❖ *His Resurrection* (Mark 16:1–8; John 11:25–26)
- ❖ *Eternal Life* (John 3:16; 10:27–29)

CLAIMING OUR IDENTITY IN CHRIST

In order to model Christ, to take hold of this awesome responsibility to our grandchildren, we need to affirm who we are in Christ. In previous chapters, we have learned how to live the role of grandparent: that we are to be the counselor, guide, teacher, and nurturer of our adult children and grandchildren. God has shown His abundant grace to us as we follow His plan of healthy love and concern for our grandchildren and have fun with them. But who are we "in Christ"?

- ❖ Are you the same person you were on that day of days when you asked Jesus to come into your heart to be Lord and Savior?

- ❖ How have you changed?
- ❖ How have you grown in the Lord?
- ❖ Who are you in Christ—right now?

Being "in Christ" as a senior adult is the same as it was on that day of days when we first accepted Jesus. Paul said it well in Galatians 2:20 (RSV): "I have been crucified with Christ; it is no longer I who live, but Christ lives in me; and the life which I now live in the flesh I live by faith in the Son of God, who loved me and gave Himself for me."

Being "in Christ" never stops. It is an ongoing part of our entire life's work. God's hope for us, indeed His instruction to us, is that we grow in intimacy with Christ as the years go by. Why do you suppose He wants us to do that? He wants us to come as close as possible to His identity.

Christ's Identity	*My Identity*	*Scripture*
The Way, the Truth, and the Life	His way, His truth, and His life	John 14:6
The Light of the world	His light to others	John 8:12
The Door to salvation	His instrument to lead others to salvation	John 10:9
The Good Shepherd	I live for others	John 10:11, 27–28
The Resurrection	I believe	1 Peter 1:3

The Bible has a great deal more to say about our identity in Christ. Because we live in the world, it can be a daily struggle to remember who we really are in Him. Adult children and grandchildren who disappoint us, poor health, financial problems, loss, old age, and other forces can create a self-centeredness that is not true to the gospel. Such external forces can cause us to deny the internal Christ. The truth is that once invited in, He never leaves us. It is we who move away from Him.

Through daily prayer, grandparents can claim their identity in Jesus Christ and live that identity with assurance. Then when we are called to heaven, we can claim the promises of our heavenly Father. Read Galatians 2:20 again and praise God for the greatest gift of all, His beloved, perfect, and redeeming Son, and the Holy Spirit living within you.

MODELING ACCORDING TO GOD'S WORD

Two ways in which grandparents can model Christ are by modeling godly traits in our daily walk and by demonstrating that we handle life experiences according to God's Word.

1. Consider these seventeen godly traits with suggested Bible passages in light of your own goals as a godly model.

Trait   *God's Word*

Humility .... Colossians 3:1–2; James 4:6
Self-discipline .... 1 Corinthians 6:12, 2 Timothy 2:4
Love .... Colossians 3:14; 1 Corinthians 13
Devotion .... Matthew 16:24; Romans 12:1
Self-sacrifice .... Philippians 2:4
Compassion .... 1 Peter 3:8
Patience .... 1 Thessalonians 5:14
Truthfulness .... Proverbs 12:22
Fairness .... Romans 12:17
Perseverance .... Galatians 6:9
Faithfulness .... 1 Corinthians 4:2
Obedience .... Deuteronomy 28:15
Respectfulness .... 1 Peter 2:17
Honesty .... Leviticus 19:35–36; Proverbs 11:20
Bravery .... Proverbs 28:1
Sharing .... Proverbs 11:25; Luke 6:38
Humor .... Proverbs 15:13; 17:22

2. Next, focus on modeling by demonstrating that you handle these life experiences according to what is taught in God's Word.

Experience	*God's Word*
Friendship	Proverbs 18:24
Marriage	Mark 10:6–9; Ephesians 5:21–25
Citizenship	Matthew 22:17–21; 1 Peter 2:13–17
Aging	Psalm 92:14; Proverbs 16:31; Titus 2:2–3
Retirement	Psalm 71:18; Isaiah 46:4; Proverbs 3:1–2
Suffering	Psalm 46:1; 73:26; Romans 8:18
Grief because of death	2 Corinthians 5:1–10; 1 Thessalonians 4:13–18

Who Is Watching and What Does It Matter?

We are saddened by stories that crop up all too often about well-known evangelists and other Christian leaders who have fallen from grace.

All the world's a stage! All the world is watching. The unsaved and the lost waiting for redemption are our responsibility. One by one, at any age, we can make a difference by standing firm for the gospel truth and modeling Christ for others.

Timothy's grandmother modeled Christ for the generations that came after her. So can we. The things we do and say in our own lifetime can make the difference in the salvation of souls.

When we reduce the world to our own sphere of influence—family, friends, community—we get a more realistic view of the importance of modeling Christ in an ungodly world. What matters to God is that we try. What is at stake is the salvation of the world.

GRACE PRINCIPLE:

God's grace can be modeled by grandparents.

Only be careful, and watch yourselves closely so that you do not forget the things your eyes have seen or let them slip from your heart as long as you live. Teach them to your children and to their children after them.

— Deuteronomy 4:9

Nothing a Christian grandparent does for the balance of his or her life is as important as the subject of the next chapter—the work of passing on our faith to our children and our children's children.

℮

Chapter 20

PASSING ON
THE FAITH

Nearer, nearer, nearer to the everlasting arms." I can still hear Grandma Burch singing that old hymn as she poured the pancake batter on the hot black surface of the wood stove.

I can still see her loosen the tattered clip from the top of her head so that her frail silver hair fell almost to the floor. She would place her store-bought teeth on a little round table, lean back in a chair, eyes closed, and hum a love song to her Lord. I remember thinking she was the most beautiful lady I had ever known. I still do.

Grandma's beauty was not in her gnarled, rough hands or her figure, expanded by childbirth and good food. It was not in her weathered, lined face, or her voice which often sought the right note in vain, or in her work for so many others. It was not even in her long, silver hair. Grandma's beauty was deep inside. It was Jesus shining His love through her.

As a young girl I was drawn to that inner beauty. I wanted to know more about this Jesus who supplied all her needs even as my Grandma lived in such primitive times of great hardship.

Who is this One who saves, sustains, and provides such contentment and grace that my grandma would be found singing His praises until the day He took her home?

That's the hunger grandparents can instill in grandchildren—to know the love of God the Father through His Son, to want to draw nearer to His throne that they might receive His grace and live in faith.

Grandparents Growing in Grace and Knowledge

To pass on God's grace to others, grandparents must continue to walk closely with Him. We will never know all there is to know about God's grace. The person who continues to learn as long as God gives life and breath *will never be old.* The person who stops learning *grows old.*

To grow in God's grace, we must be in God's Word. Make time in each day for personal Bible study. It's never too late to commit to a Bible study group, one at church or a home Bible study for neighbors and friends. The Bible is our Heavenly Father's journal in which divinely inspired writers tell about the wondrous gifts He waits to freely give his children. We have but to open this journal, read it faithfully, believe, and receive. If this is an area in your Christian walk that has been neglected in recent years, now is a good time to make a renewed commitment to making Bible study a top priority in your day. Everyone can benefit from searching and storing the Word of God.

To grow in God's grace, we must pray without ceasing. What does Paul mean to "pray without ceasing"? In practical terms, that is probably not possible unless one lives in a monastery, with every waking moment devoted to prayer. What do we who would follow in the steps of Christians who have prayed before us hear Paul asking us to do?

Most of us grew to grandparenting with a tradition of prayer that includes "Now I lay me down to sleep" and the Lord's Prayer, or praying a prayer of thanksgiving, or for a specific need in a particular situation. Many grandparents have a real longing for prayer, especially when we see other lives touched at a deep level by prayer. Often that longing comes from a restlessness, a feeling that God seems far away.

To pray without ceasing means to make prayer a way of life. Roberta Bondi writes in her book, *To Pray and To Love,* "Prayer, like love, as a way of life is not something that comes to us ready-made, simply by deciding we want it. We learn it with the help of the Holy Spirit *over a lifetime* by practicing it, pondering it, and using the resources, including Scripture, that other Christians have passed on to us."

Pray with the expectation that God is waiting to hear from you. He is. Pray for God's will to be done. Thank Him for all that He has done, is doing, and will yet do for you and your beloved family. "The effectual fervent prayer of a righteous man availeth much" (Jas. 5:16, KJV).

To grow in God's grace, we must take time to listen to God. An old friend of mine tells a revealing story. It begins with the discovery of one unexpected hour one day in which she had nothing to do.

Gleefully, she decided that the hour would be dedicated to prayer! She began with praise, then thanksgiving. That didn't seem quite enough. There was a strange stirring, a discontent with the entire effort.

Continuing, she asked God's will in matters concerning her work and her grandchildren. There it was again! A funny feeling in her spirit. Stopping in the middle of her prayers, she said aloud, "This just isn't working very well!" Then she asked an important question. "What is it you would have me do with this gift of time that I have dedicated to you?" And God said, "Child of Mine, be still and let Me love you." Allow God to speak to you, revealing His marvelous love to your heart.

To grow in knowledge, we must stay active in the church. God honors the one who comes forward when there is a need in the church family, however small. The one who says, "I'll serve, I'll try, I'll help" will continue to grow and find that each day holds new excitement, new opportunities. Fulfill the roles your physical self will allow.

To grow in knowledge, we must stay active in the community. There is a need, greater than ever before, for seniors to speak boldly for Christian values, to quiet those who would destroy the foundations upon which our country was founded. Serve your fellow man, regardless of race, color, or creed, with compassion, understanding, and Christian love.

To grow in knowledge, we must stay active in the family. Grandparents are at the center of the family. Children, grandchildren, and great-grandchildren need to know they can always depend on their grandparents to be a treasure house of history, tradition, and wisdom and a model for the Christian life.

It's Never Too Late

to be a disciple of Christ,
not an imitation of Christ.

to pass on the gospel Truth
as long as God gives life and breath.

to be a blessing to another
by prayer, caring, or touching.

to make a contribution
to the eternal salvation of another.

to find the joy
in the grandparenting season.

to accept God's unconditional love,
mercy, and grace.

Principles to Pass On

Throughout this book, we have spoken of Grace Principles. Most of us have always known God's grace as God's favor extended continuously toward the lost and the saved.

Lost persons experience God's graciousness as *saving grace:*

Saved persons experience God's gift as *sustaining grace* that restores fellowship, empowers for ministry, and strengthens for daily challenges.

<u>Sustaining Grace:</u>

- ❖ *It is a gift freely given!* "The Spirit and the bride say, 'Come!' And let him who hears say, 'Come!' Whoever is thirsty, let him come; and whoever wishes, let him take the free gift of the water of life" (Rev. 22:17). God closes the Bible with invitation. In His final appeal, He is saying sinners still have time. What encouragement that offers grandparents who have not yet received Christ!

- ❖ *We cannot earn it!* "He saved us, not because of deeds done by us in righteousness, but in virtue of his own mercy, by the washing of regeneration and renewal in the Holy Spirit, which he poured out upon us richly through Jesus Christ our Savior, so that we might be justified by his grace and become heirs in hope of eternal life" (Titus 3:5–7, RSV).

- ❖ *We don't deserve it!* "But because of his great love for us, God, who is rich in mercy, made us alive with Christ even when we were dead in transgressions—it is by grace you have been saved" (Eph. 2:4–5).

- ❖ *It comes from God!* "For the Lord God is a sun and shield; The LORD gives grace and glory; No good thing does he withhold from those who walk uprightly" (Ps. 84:11, NASB).

- ❖ *It is available to every believer!* "Let us therefore draw near with confidence to the throne of grace, that we may receive mercy and may find grace to help in time of need" (Heb. 4:16, NASB).

❖ *It is sufficient!* "'My grace is sufficient for you, for my power is made perfect in weakness'" (2 Cor. 12:9, RSV).

ACCEPTING GOD'S GRACE

In order to pass on our faith to present and future generations, we need to have accepted God's grace personally.

In the Good Times

Dorothy and Edgar have been married thirty-three years and are in good health. They have two successful children and five perfect grandchildren. All of their children and grandchildren are walking with the Lord and credit Grandma and Grandpa with reinforcing their deep faith in God.

Now, have Dorothy and Edgar lived a "charmed" life without bends in the road, disappointments, and problems? No. But by concentrating not on the negatives, but giving thanks for all of the blessings of their lives as a living testimony to God's goodness, they have succeeded mightily!

In Times of Loss

Mary and John were married fifty-one years. They had many good friends and a loving family. Friends and family surrounded Mary after John passed away. Mary, overcome with grief at her loss, rejected the love. She remained reclusive and despondent until her death. She missed God's blessings that come in the certain valleys of this life.

After Sinning

Edward knows his habits of smoking and drinking beer are offensive and dangerous to himself, his wife, and their long marriage. He knows in his heart that his offenses are the reasons the grandchildren do not come to visit. He is convicted to quit but doesn't want to admit his weakness.

We claim for Edward, Hebrews 10:16–17, "This is the covenant I will make with them after that time, says the Lord.

I will put my laws in their hearts and I will write them on their minds." Then He adds, "Your sins and lawless acts I will remember no more."

In the Twilight of Life

Louella has occupied the same pew in the same church for sixty years. She recently admitted to her pastor that she was not certain of her salvation and was afraid to die. For Louella, here are the words of peace and joy from Romans 5:1–2: "Therefore, since we have been justified through faith, we have peace with God through our Lord Jesus Christ, through whom we have gained access by faith into this grace in which we now stand. And we rejoice in the hope of the glory of God."

As recipients of grace so great, how can we pass it on to children and grandchildren? We must never let a generation miss the knowledge of God's gift because of us. That is our responsibility.

We can accomplish our job by example in everyday living and during those special moments with those we love. We can speak it, journal it for the generations that follow, and model and teach the truth of God's grace, even as we have fun with our grandchildren.

GRACE PRINCIPLE:

We are to pass on God's grace.

Each one should use whatever gift he has received to serve others, faithfully administering God's grace in its various forms.

— 1 Peter 4:10

We will now take an honest look at the legacy we are leaving our grandchildren. Is it temporal, or is it eternal?

℮

Chapter 21

A GRANDPARENT'S
LEGACY

Grandma Charlotte was a saver. She had a basement filled with a lifetime of "things" she might use "some day." There were no less than three cedar chests packed with sets of silverware fit for a king, brass and gold candle holders, and two complete china services for twelve. Over the years she would take pieces out of the chest from time to time to look at them, and then put them back in their safe place, hidden away.

One winter night when Grandma Charlotte was away, thieves broke into the house and carried out the chests with their valuable contents. None of the loss was ever recovered.

Nettie was a saver, too. The attic in her home was a treasure house of memories from her life and the lives of her eight children and seventeen grandchildren. The attic door was always open. Any day any number of grown and growing kids walked through that door to pore over the legacy of love and faith that was their great gift from Grandma Nettie: faded pictures in boxes, programs from school events long ago, dozens of church bulletins with their names in them, a cheerleading megaphone standing in the corner, a wooden cradle Grandpa made in which almost all of the children had slept in their infancy, old Bibles which had been "loaned" to little ones who practiced Grandma Nettie's own special methods of Scripture memorization. These were treasures they could touch as they relived a memory with much joy and sometimes . a tear.

Of what value were Grandma Charlotte's cedar chests?

Of what value were Grandma Nettie's attic treasures?

The things of the world are not ours. They are graciously apportioned to us. What we do with them is up to us and is a measure of our Christian walk and the legacy we leave for others.

The question we can now ask ourselves is this: What legacy are we leaving our grandchildren? Is it temporal, or is it eternal? Is it a legacy of "things" or a legacy of faith, hope, and godliness? We will be remembered by the life we lived. It is never too late to begin again.

A LEGACY OF UNFINISHED BUSINESS

Some grandparents deeply regret the blemishes on the legacy they will leave their children and grandchildren, mistakes that have been made—mistakes still mired in denial or the absence of forgiveness. But our gracious God encourages new beginnings, even for grandparents!

The Bible says in Exodus that the sins of the fathers are passed on to the children through the third and fourth generation. This happens not because God doesn't love grandchildren, but because it is a basic principle of human nature. When you sin, your children learn from your sin and their children from theirs. That sin can be passed on by example until the cycle is broken.

Godly grandparents break that cycle by taking an honest look at unwritten rules that keep the dysfunction going. Unfinished business, left alone, harms others. How can a new beginning come about? Similar to reversing unhealthy concern that results in meddling, the grandparent in denial must:

1. Stop blaming. Own the problem. As long as you are in the blaming department, you will never get out.
2. Take responsibility for your past, present, and future actions.
3. Repent earnestly. Take authority over what has happened and ask God's forgiveness.[1] "If we confess our sins, he is faithful and just and will forgive us our sins and purify us from all unrighteousness" (1 John 1:9).
4. Ask forgiveness of the loved ones you have wronged.

A Legacy of Blessing

Dr. Mary Ruth Swope of Phoenix, Arizona, received a legacy of blessing from her grandmother which she is passing on today to her grandson, Daniel. As a girl, Mary Ruth's grandmother had read her stories, said prayers with her, helped her memorize Scripture, and played games. When Mary Ruth became a grandmother, she remembered the blessings bestowed upon her life by her loving grandmother and asked God for a way to pass them on to Daniel.

Scripture reminded her in Genesis 49:28 that when Jacob was old, he called together his twelve sons. "He blessed them, every one with a blessing appropriate to him." Our Lord Jesus provides the best example of how to bless our children. When several parents brought their children to Him, "He took the children in his arms, put his hands on them and blessed them" (Mark 10:13–16).

Mary Ruth embarked upon a grandparent mission to bless grandson Daniel and has witnessed changes in his life that conform with the words of her spoken and written blessings. We can do the same for our grandchildren. Here's how it works: Commit to a specific, consistent daily or weekly blessing for your grandchild. If your grandchild lives close by, speak it. If your grandchild lives far away, write it. For inspiration, here are a few sample blessings for grandchildren from Dr.

Mary Ruth Swope's powerful little book, *Bless Your Children Every Day* .

Assurance:

In the name of Jesus Christ, I bless you with the assurance that God will seek for you if you are lost and will bind you up if you are broken and will strengthen you if you are sick. Indeed, He will always be seeking you as one of His sheep and will deliver you to a safe place if you wander off the right pathway. You may be sure that God will do what He has promised.

Authority:

In the name of Jesus Christ, I bless you with the revelation that God has given you authority over all the power of the enemy and nothing will harm you. No weapon formed against you will prosper. Do not fear, therefore, or be afraid. You can be victorious over the enemy. It is God's will to deliver you.

Clear Direction:

In the name of Jesus Christ, I bless your going out and your coming in today and every day. May you ponder the way of your feet and not turn to the right or to the left from the path that God has planned for you. May you understand the lessons He is trying to teach you from what He permits to happen in your life. If you stay on God's pathway, your life will be filled with joy and gladness.[2]

A covenant to bless your grandchild(ren) regularly can bring about changes not only in the life of the child, but also in the lives of other family members who observe those changes. Imagine the joy Mary Ruth receives when her grandson asks, "Grandmother, are you going to bless me today?"

A LEGACY OF HEROISM

Grandfathers are naturally heroic figures to most children. Being a hero doesn't necessarily mean that you were the first man on the moon. In the eyes of a grandchild, a grandfather is half real, half fantasy, a real-life figure of which legends are created.

You can hear the hero worship when a grandchild talks about his grandfather. "My grandpa worked in a mine when he was young and he showed me some nuggets he dug up there!" "My grandpa can fix anything. He has more tools than anybody in the world!"

Grandfathers are not only revered by kids for their stories of the distant past but by their current deeds as well. Kids like to point to their grandfather's job, his role in the community or in the military, his leadership ability, and his religious life. When there is a close, intimate relationship between grandfather and grandchild, there is a tendency on the part of the child to take what Grandpa says and does as gospel. That's part of the responsibility that comes with being a hero and makes it all the more important to be a positive and not a negative role model for the child.

A grandfather's elevated status also provides a platform for the passing on of values and Christian principles. Grandfather can be the teacher of a curriculum not taught in school. His classroom is portable. It is anywhere he is together with his grandchild. Grandfathers can impart information and ethics a child can learn nowhere else.

And grandfathers can turn the tables on their grandkids in a beautiful way. One grandfather told me, "Shucks, I'm not the hero in this relationship. My little grandson is! Why, he teaches me something every time I'm with him!" This grandfather waxes eloquently about the boy's activities and accomplishments, taking every opportunity to build his self-esteem. Now, that's what I call heroic!

Sometimes a grandfather can be a hero just by taking time out to be with a grandchild. Eight-year-old Teddy loves to stay overnight at his grandparents' house because Grandma always makes such good dinners. (Except for her spaghetti. Teddy gives Grandma's spaghetti a rating of four, after his mother's, his aunt's, and his best friend's mother's. (*Oh, well. You can't win them all.*)

One night, as Grandma came to tuck Teddy in and give him a kiss on the forehead, Grandpa walked by the door. Teddy called to him, "Grandpa, could you stay with me for a while?" Grandpa, who had not yet finished his newspaper, almost said no. But he glanced in at the boy and saw something in his eyes that said, "This is important."

Grandpa stretched out on the bed next to Teddy, who lay on his side with his arm across his Grandpa's chest. They talked about school and a few other things. Finally, Grandpa said, "Was there something special you wanted to talk about, partner?" "No," said Teddy. "I just wanted you to be with me."

That touched Grandpa. What could be more important than spending time with a child who wanted to be with him? He realized that too soon Teddy will outgrow that need, and Grandpa will be begging to spend a little time with him!

The grandfather who takes the time to be with a grandchild is the best kind of hero.

THE STORY OF ELI CREEKMORE

Myrna Struchen-Johnson's grandson, Eli, lived in a violent home. Myrna worried constantly about Eli's safety. When she saw Eli, he had bruises, cuts, and cigarette burns on his body. Despite his sad life, Eli always had a big smile for his grandma. Myrna made more than one hundred calls to social service agencies requesting they investigate the home, fearing for the very life of her grandson.

Her darkest fears were realized September 27, 1986, when her only grandson died at the age of three years, one month, and nine days, kicked in the stomach by his father.

Three days after Eli's death, crowds of people gathered on the state capital steps, inspired by Eli's grandmother, to protest state policies that allowed Eli Creekmore to remain in his abusive home. Eli's death set in motion a wave of public outrage.

The trial of Darren Creekmore dragged on as he remained in jail and Myrna led the fight for a stronger law against abusers. Finally, almost three years later, in 1989, a new Washington state law, "Homicide By Abuse" was passed by the legislature, making abuse an automatic first degree murder charge. Darren Creekmore was sentenced to sixty years in prison.

One grandmother's relentless battle for justice was over. Because of her individual efforts, other states began to look seriously at their own laws against child abuse. Myrna had created a legacy for her grandson and for all children who live in abusive home environments.

How great is God's grace? Like so many across the nation who watched the aftermath of this tragedy unfold, I was moved by the far-reaching legacy of this courageous grandmother. In that last newspaper story was a picture of the grandmother holding a framed portrait of her lost grandson, Eli. The headline over the picture read something like, "It Will Never Be Over for This Grandmother." Myrna had fought for years for legislation to protect children in Washington state from abuse, and she had won. Still, she mourned for her only grandson, Eli. At the time, I was just beginning to write a new book on grandparenting. For inspiration, I cut out Myrna's picture from the newspaper and taped it to my computer. For two years, every day I worked on the book, I saw Myrna's picture and sent up an "arrow prayer" that God might some day replace her loss with joy.

Two years later, still praying for Myrna, I was interviewing a young woman, Lauri Starkovich, on my radio program in Seattle. In my guest's lap was a six-month-old Romanian boy she had recently adopted. I asked his name. Lauri said he was named Eli for Eli Creekmore, who had died by the violence of his father. She told us that she and her husband, unable to have a child, had promised God that if given a boy to raise, they would bring him up to know the Lord and name him for the little boy who didn't have a chance at life.

I was shocked! During the commercial break, I told the mother I had been praying for Eli Creekmore's grandmother for more than two years that God would replace her loss with joy. Lauri was moved to tears. "Do you know her?" she asked. I told Lauri no, but promised that if ever I met Myrna, I would let her know.

One year later, in a completely unrelated incident, I was auditing a grandparent support group meeting, making notes for an article I was writing about grandparents who were raising their own grandchildren. I had been introduced by the group leader as one who was writing about their situation. At the end of the meeting, a woman came toward me in the half light, leaned down and said, "I'm glad you are writing about this. I'm here with my neighbor who is raising her grandson. I lost mine."

Suddenly, I realized that I was looking into the face in the newspaper story, the face of the grandmother for whom I had been praying for almost three years.

I exclaimed, "Myrna?" "Yes," she said, clutching her hand to her breast. We sat down and talked. I told her about the very special little boy living close by who was named for her grandson, Eli. Would she like to meet him? "Would I?" she exclaimed.

Early the next morning I called Lauri, who was elated at the news! We made a date for the following Wednesday afternoon. On that day, Lauri, her son, Eli, and I traveled to Myrna Struchen-Johnson's home where, in one hour, God knit together the remnants of a grandmother's grief.

When we arrived, Eli went right to Myrna who lifted him into her arms, tears streaming down her face. In Myrna's living room, Eli played with wooden toys Eli Creekmore's grandfather had made for his own grandson. We discovered Eli liked to hit pots and pans with wooden spoons just as Eli Creekmore had. It was a privilege to observe and feel the joy, to witness firsthand the grace of God.

God had been at work in all of our lives for more than three years.

❖ He honored the prayer of a stranger who had prayed for another stranger for three years.
❖ He honored the prayer of a barren young couple who desperately wanted a baby.
❖ He saved a baby from deprivation and almost certain death in a Romanian orphanage.
❖ He empowered one grandmother to leave a legacy of love that will impact perhaps millions of grandchildren in future years.
❖ He replaced her loss with joy.

I hope you will remember the story of Eli Creekmore and the faithfulness of our gracious God. Remember it especially at those times in the dark valleys of your life. For God is in control. He makes beauty from the ashes. He wrote the legacy Myrna left in the name of her grandson.

GRACE PRINCIPLE:

It is never too late to accept God's grace.

"And surely I am with you always, to the very end of the age."
— Matthew 28:20

℮

GRACE PRINCIPLES BY CHAPTER

Chapter One:
God's grace sustains us.

Chapter Two:
Good grandparents learn by God's grace.

Chapter Three:
God's grace is evident in children and grandchildren.

Chapter Four:
We cannot earn God's grace.

Chapter Five:
God's grace brings responsibility.

Chapter Six:
Grace is God's favor extended to every believer.

Chapter Seven:
God's grace awaits the repentent sinner.

Chapter Eight:
We do not deserve God's grace.

Chapter Nine:
God's grace is a source of joy.

Chapter Ten:
By God's grace, joy is preserved.

Chapter Eleven:
God's grace is a gift.

Chapter Twelve:
God's grace is unconditional.

Chapter Thirteen:
Future generations need God's grace.

Chapter Fourteen:
We will always need God's grace.

Chapter Fifteen:
God's grace is real.

Chapter Sixteen:
God's grace is sufficient.

Chapter Seventeen:
God's grace is free.

Chapter Eighteen:
God precisely fits his grace to the need of the recipient.

Chapter Nineteen:
God's grace can be modeled by grandparents.

Chapter Twenty:
We are to pass on God's grace.

Chapter Twenty-one:
It is never too late to accept God's grace.

NOTES

Chapter 1

1. Judith Waldrop, "The Grandbaby Boom," *American Demographics,* September 1993, 4.

2. "Population Reports: Marital Status and Living Arrangements," series P–20, no. 450, U.S. Department of Commerce, March 1990, 4.

Chapter 3

1. Arthur Kornhaber, *Between Parents and Grandparents* (New York: St. Martin's Press, 1986), 144–45.

Chapter 4

1. Cecil A. Ray, *Living the Responsible Life, Profiles of the Christian Steward* (Nashville: Convention Press, 1974), 1.

2. Irene M. Endicott, *Grandparenting Redefined, Guidance for Today's Changing Family* (Lynnwood, Wash.: Aglow Publications, 1992), 147–48.

3. "Give a Child a Giftrust" (1993) Twentieth Century Services, Inc., P.O. Box 419200, Kansas City, Mo. 64141-6200.

4. "Generation Skipping Trust" (GST), *Executive Table Talk* (Lansing, Mich.: Jackson National Life Insurance), 4.

5. George D. Brenner, "Coping with the Finances of Educating Children," *Journal of the American Society of CLU and ChFC,* March 1990, 58.

6. Willliam G. Brennan, "Putting the Children in a Home of Their Own," *Financial World,* December 1992, 1.

7. Richard B. Cunningham, *Resource Unlimited, Christian Stewardship—From Theology to Ecology, from Motives to Methods.* ed. William L. Hendricks, (Nashville: Southern Baptist Convention Stewardship Commission, 1972), 233.

8. Barbara Deane, *Getting Ready For A Great Retirement, A Planning Guide* (Colorado Springs: NavPress, 1992), 166.

9. Endicott,*Grandparenting Redefined,* 150, 151.

Chapter 5

1. Stephen and Janet Bly, *How To Be A Good Grandparent,* (Chicago: Moody Press, 1990), 66.

Chapter 6

1. William Lee Carter, "The Oppositional Child," Kid Think, (Houston; Dallas: Rapha Publishing/Word, Inc., 1991), 3.

Chapter 8

1. T.W. Hunt, "His Love," *The Mind of Christ,* (Nashville: Southern Baptist Convention Sunday School Board, 1992), 11.

Chapter 9

1. Judy Gattis Smith, *Grandmother Time,* (Dallas: Word Kids! Word Publishing, 1991), 22–23.

Chapter 10

1. Irene M. Endicott, *Out of the Mouths of Grandchildren,* (Nashville: Family Touch Press, 1993).

Chapter 12

1. *Montana Star Bulletin,* April 24, 1948.

Chapter 15

1. Mothers Against Drunk Driving, (MADD), 511 E. John Carpenter Freeway, Suite 700, Irving, Tex. 75062-8187, (214) 744-6233.

2. National Center for Health Statistics, 301-436-8979.

3. Mothers Against Violence in America (MAVIA), P O Box 444, Mercer Island, WA 98040-0444, 206-343-0676.

4. James J. McKenna, "SIDS Research," *MOTHERING*, Winter 1992, 45.

5. "Acquired Immunodeficiency Syndrome—United States." Centers For Disease Control and Prevention, U.S. Department of Health and Human Services Morbidity and Mortality Weekly Report, vol. 42, no. 28, July 23, 1993, 547–551, 557,

Chapter 16

1. "Marital Status andLiving Arrangements," Population Characteristics, U.S. Bureau of the Census, Series P-20, no. 461, March 1991.

2. "Generations," *The Detroit Free Press*, March 12, 1994, 9-D.

3. American Association of Retired Persons, (AARP) Board Byline, vol. 6, no. 1, Winter 1992–1993, 1, 3.

4. Grandparents Raising Grandchildren, Inc., Pacific Northwest Region, 20227 87th Avenue W., Edmonds, Wash. 98026

5. Grandparents Support Network, May/June 1993 Newsletter, 208 66th Avenue E., Tacoma, Wash. 98424.

Chapter 17

1. Endicott, "Grandparents' Rights," *Grandparenting Redefined, 108.*

2. Ibid., 109.

3. Greenville County Department of Social Services vs. Bowes, et al, Judge A. J. Toal, Supreme Court of the State of South Carolina, October 1993, 45–46.

Chapter 18

1. Richard S. Victor, "Grandparents andOther Third Party Rights," Grandparents Rights Organization (GRO) newsletter, vol. 5, no. 1, 1–5.

2. Ibid.

Chapter 21

1. Endicott, *Grandparenting Redefined*, 170–71.

2. Mary Ruth Swope, *Bless Your Children Every Day,* (Phoenix: Swope Enterprises 1992)

RESOURCES

Books

Aldrich, Robert A. *Grandparenting for the Nineties.* San Marcos, Calif.: Robert Erdmann Publishing, 1991.

Aliki. *The Two of Them.* New York: Greenwillow Books, 1979.

Arthur, Kay. *Lord, I Need Grace to Make It.* Portland, Oreg.: Multnomah Press, 1989.

Bly, Stephen and Janet. *How to Be a Good Grandparent.* Chicago: Moody Press, 1990.

Bondi, Roberta C. *To Pray & To Love.* Minneapolis: Augsburg Fortress, 1991.

Bridges, Jerry. *The Practice of Godliness.* Colorado Springs: NavPress, 1983.

Carter, William Lee. *Kid Think.* Houston: Rapha Publishing/WORD, Inc., 1991.

Chapman, Steve and Annie. *Gifts Your Kids Can't Break.* Minneapolis: Bethany House Publishers, 1991.

Cherlin, Andrew J. *The New American Grandparent, A Place in the Family.* Cambridge, Mass.: Harvard University Press, 1992.

Coleman, William. *How to Go Home Without Feeling Like a Child.* Houston: Word Publishing, 1991.

Comer, James P. *Raising Black Children.* New York: Penguin Books, 1992.

Cook, Melva. *Coping with Crisis in the Senior Years.* Nashville: Convention Press, 1992.

Coontz, Stephanie. *The Way We Never Were.* New York: Basic Books, 1992.

Curb, Dolph L., Ben E. Dickerson, Carolyn D. Spears, Robert W. Trotter. *Growing Older, Growing Wiser.* Nashville: Family Touch Press, 1993.

Deane, Barbara. *Getting Ready for a Great Retirement.* Colorado Springs: NavPress, 1992.

DePaola, Tomie. *Now, One Foot, Now the Other.* New York: G. P. Putman, 1981.

Endicott, Irene M. *Grandparenting Redefined, Guidance for Today's Changing Family.* Lynnwood, Wash.: Aglow Publications, 1992.

————. *Out of the Mouths of Grandchildren.* Nashville: Family Touch, 1993.

George, Denise. *God's Gentle Whisper.* Lynnwood, Wash.: Aglow Publications, 1994.

Gibson, Dennis and Ruth. *The Sandwich Years.* Grand Rapids: Baker Book House Company, 1991.

Hendricks, William L. *Resource Unlimited.* Nashville: The Southern Baptist Convention Stewardship Commission, 1972.

Kornhaber, Arthur. *Between Parents and Grandparents.* New York: St. Martin's Press, 1986.

Lasky, Kathryn. *I Have Four Names for My Grandfather.* Boston: Little, Brown & Co., 1976.

MacLachlan, Patricia. *Through Grandpa's Eyes.* New York: Harper & Row, 1979.

Minkler, Meredith and Kathleen M. Roe. *Grandmothers as Caregivers.* Newbury Park, Calif.: Sage Publications, 1993.

Ortlund, Anne. *Disciplines of the Home.* Houston: Word Publishing, 1990.

Ray, Cecil A. *Living the Responsible Life.* Nashville: Convention Press, 1974.

Schreur, Jerry and Jack. *Creative Grandparenting.* Grand Rapids, Mich.: Discovery Publishing, 1992.

Smith, Joanne and Judy Biggs. *How to Say Goodbye.* Lynnwood, Wash.: Aglow Publications, 1990.

Smith, Judy Gattis. *Grandmother Time.* Houston: Word Kids, 1991.

Stern, Kenneth A. *Senior Savvy, to Preserve, Control & Maximize Your Estate.* San Diego, Calif.: Segue Capital, Inc.

Stoop, Jan and Betty Southard. *The Grandmother Book.* Nashville: Thomas Nelson Publishers, 1993.

Swope, Mary Ruth. *Bless Your Children Every Day.* Swope Enterprises, Inc., 1992.

Vigna, Judith. *Grandma Without Me.* Morton Grove, Ill.: Albert Whitman & Company, 1984.

Williams, Barbara. *Kevin's Grandma.* New York: Dutton Children's Books, 1975.

Zolotow, Charlotte. *I Know a Lady.* New York: Puffin Books, 1984.

Support Groups

Grandparenting by Grace Support Groups
    Discipleship & Family Development Dept.
    Sunday School Board, Southern Baptist Convention
    127 9th Ave. N.
    Nashville, TN 37234
    615-251-2280

AARP Grandparent Information Center,
    601 E. Street NW
    Washington, DC 20049
    202-434-2296

R.O.C.K.I.N.G., Inc. (Raising Our Children's Kids)
    P. O. Box 96
    Niles, MI 49120
    616-683-9038

The Children's Defense Fund
    25 E. Street NW
    Washington, DC 20001
    202-628-8787

Grandparents Raising Grandchildren, Inc. (GRG)
    20227 87th Ave. W
    Edmonds, WA 98026
    206-774-9721

Second Time Around Parents (STAP)
    100 W. Front St.
    Media, PA 19063
    217-566-7540

Columbia Health Center
    4400 37th Ave. S.
    Seattle, WA 98144
    206-296-4650

Grandparents as Parents (GAP)
    3536 S. Mitchell
    Boise, ID 83709
    208-362-9044

Grandparents as Parents (GAP)
    2801 Atlantic Ave.
    Long Beach, CA 90801
    310-933-3151

Grandparents Raising Grandchildren (GRG)
    P.O. Box 104
    Colleyville, TX 76034
    817-577-0435

Grandparents as Parents (GAP)
    53 Lisa Lane
    Lowell, MA 01854
    508-454-6303

For support group information in your area, contact your local county Area Agency on Aging.

Grandparent Rights
    Grandparent Rights Organization (GRO)
    555 S. Woodward, Suite 600
    Birmingham, MI 48009
    313-646-7191

Grandparents' Rights Advocacy Movement, Inc.
    P.O. Box 523
    Tarpon Springs, FL 34688-0523
    813-937-2317